X 45

Air War
Northern Ireland

Air War Northern Ireland

Britain's Air Arms and the 'Bandit Country'
of South Armagh

Operation BANNER 1969-2007

Steven Taylor

Pen & Sword
AVIATION

First published in Great Britain in 2018
and reprinted in this format in 2022 by
Pen & Sword Aviation
an imprint of
Pen & Sword Books Ltd
47 Church Street
Barnsley
South Yorkshire
S70 2AS

ISBN 9-781-39902-037-4

A CIP catalogue entry for this book is available from the British Library.

Typeset in INDIA by Geniies IT & Services Private Limited.

Printed and bound by CPI Group (UK) Ltd, Croydon, CR0 4YY

Pen & Sword Books Ltd includes the Imprints of Pen & Sword
Aviation, Pen & Sword Family History, Pen & Sword Maritime,
Pen & Sword Military, Wharncliffe Local History, Pen & Sword Select,
Pen & Sword Military Classics, Leo Cooper, The Praetorian Press,
Remember When, Seaforth Publishing and Frontline Publishing.

For a complete list of Pen & Sword titles please contact
PEN & SWORD BOOKS LIMITED
47 Church Street, Barnsley, South Yorkshire, S70 2AS, England
E-mail: enquiries@pen-and-sword.co.uk
Website: www.pen-and-sword.co.uk

Contents

Acknowledgements

For their assistance with official records and historical information, I wish to thank the staff at the National Archives, Kew; the RAF Air Historical Branch; 38 (Irish) Brigade; the MoD's Army Secretariat; and the Police Service of Northern Ireland.

For permission to quote extracts from published sources, I would like to thank The O'Brien Press Ltd (*Insider* and *Enemy of the Empire*); Routledge (*British Generals in Blair's Wars* © Jonathan Bailey, Richard Iron and Hew Strachan, 2013); *Flight International* magazine (extract reproduced with permission of Reed Business Information Limited via PLSclear); HarperCollins Publishers Ltd (*Hellfire* © Ed Macy, 2009); Guy Warner (*Sycamores Over Ulster*); Headline (*Heroes of the Skies* © 2012 MAA Publishing Ltd. Extracts reproduced by permission of Headline Publishing Group); Imperial War Museum, London (various sound archives); Pan Macmillan (*Northern Ireland: Soldiers Talking* © Max Arthur, 1987. Extracts reproduced with permission of Pan Macmillan via PLSclear); Duncan Rogers of Helion & Company (*A Long Long War* and *Wasted Years, Wasted Lives - The British Army in Northern Ireland Vol. 2*); Stuart Leasor (*Rats: The Story of a Dog Soldier*); and Bloomsbury Publishing Plc (*Provos: The IRA and Sinn Fein* © Peter Taylor, 1997).

My thanks are also due to the following for their kind permission to use the illustrations featured in this book: The International Auster Club; Eamon Melaugh; Tony Crowley and the Claremont Colleges Digital Archive – Murals of Northern Ireland; David Townsend; Donald MacLeod; Museum of Army Flying; the Airborne Assault Archives, Duxford; www.flyingmarines.com; Victor Patterson; and BAe Systems.

Finally, I wish to thank Richard Doherty and the team at Pen & Sword.

Image Credits

1. Map of Northern Ireland (© Queen Mary University of London)
2. Bristol F2B (public domain)
3. Auster WE551 (© The International Auster Club)
4. Westland Sioux AH1 over Londonderry, 1972
    (© Eamon Melaugh)
5. GPMG-armed Westland Sioux AH1
    (Courtesy of flyingmarines.com)
6. Bessbrook Mill (© Museum of Army Flying)
7. DHC-2 Beaver AL1 (© BAE Systems)
8. Aerospatiale Gazelle AH1 (Courtesy of flyingmarines.com)
9. IRA volunteers manning Browning M2 (© Victor Patterson)
10. Westland Wessex HC2 XR506 (© Aviation Photo Company)
11. Test-firing of FIM-92 Stinger (© US Department of Defense)
12. Russian DShK 12.7mm heavy machine gun (iStock)
13. Mural of Lynx being shot down (© Tony Crowley)
14. Westland Lynx hovering over South Armagh field
    (© Museum of Army Flying)
15. View of 'Romeo' watchtower from door gunner's position
    (© Airborne Assault Archives, Duxford)
16. Britten-Norman Islander AL1 (© David Townsend)
17. Boeing Chinook HC2 airlifting section of watchtower
    (© Donald MacLeod)

Map

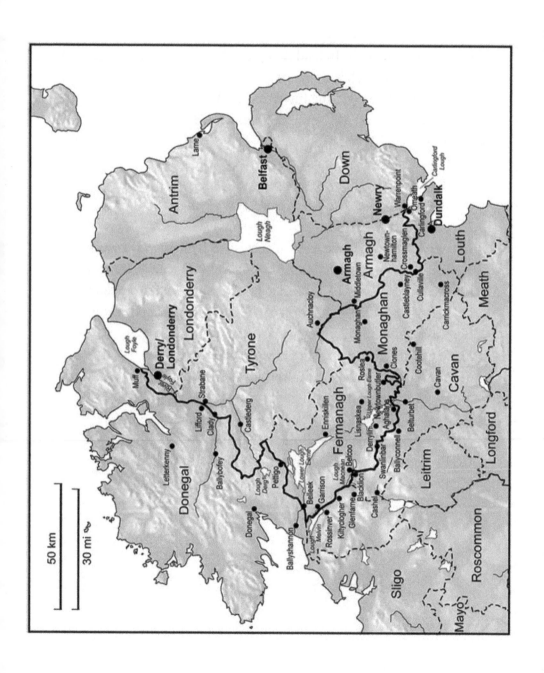

Glossary

AAC	Army Air Corps
A/C	Aircraft
AFC	Air Force Cross
AFM	Air Force Medal
ARF	Airborne Reaction Force
ASU	Active Service Unit (IRA)
ATO	Ammunition Technical Officer
AVRE	Armoured Vehicle Royal Engineers
Bn	Battalion
Brick	Four-man British Army patrol
CASEVAC	Casualty evacuation
3 CBAS	3 Commando Brigade Air Squadron
CO	Commanding Officer
COP	Close Observation Platoon
Dáil	Dáil Éireann, the lower house of the Irish legislature
DFC	Distinguished Flying Cross
DFM	Distinguished Flying Medal
Dicker	IRA look-out
DShK	Russian-made 12.7mm heavy machine gun
DSO	Distinguished Service Order
ECM	Electronic Counter Measures
EOD	Explosive Ordnance Disposal
Garda	Police force of the Republic of Ireland
GOC	General Officer Commanding
GPMG	General Purpose Machine Gun
HLS	Helicopter Landing Site
HMG	Heavy Machine Gun
HQNI	Headquarters Northern Ireland

IED	Improvised Explosive Device
IVCP	Illegal Vehicle Check Point
MANPADS	Man Portable Air Defence System
MiD	Mention in Despatches
NAS	Naval Air Squadron
NIO	Northern Ireland Office
OC	Officer Commanding
OP	Observation Post
ORB	Operations Record Book
PIRA	Provisional Irish Republican Army
PR	Photo Reconnaissance
PVCP	Permanent Vehicle Check Point
PSNI	Police Service of Northern Ireland
RIC	Reconnaissance Intelligence Centre
RPG	Rocket-Propelled Grenade
RUC	Royal Ulster Constabulary
SAM	Surface-to-Air Missile
SF	Security Forces
SH	Support Helicopters
SHDNI	Support Helicopter Detachment Northern Ireland
SHFNI	Support Helicopter Force Northern Ireland
SLR	Self-Loading Rifle
Sunray	Radio call sign for British Army unit commander
Taoiseach	Irish Prime Minister
TAOR	Tactical Area of Responsibility
UDR	Ulster Defence Regiment
USL	Underslung Load
VCP	Vehicle Check Point
Volunteer	Member of IRA
WO2	Warrant Officer Class 2
Yellow Card	Instructions on rules of engagement issued to all British soldiers serving in Northern Ireland

Prologue

The Aérospatiale Gazelle skimmed over the fields of South Armagh, flying at a height of just fifty feet. The rolling countryside flashing below was some of the most scenic in the British Isles, but the officer sitting in the observer's seat of the sleek helicopter, Lieutenant Colonel Ian Corden-Lloyd, wasn't interested in taking in the sights. Instead, his mind was firmly focused on reaching the village of Jonesborough, just a few hundred metres from the border with the Irish Republic.

The 39-year-old commanding officer of the 2nd Bn Royal Green Jackets was regarded as a rising star in the British Army. Born in Durban, South Africa, he was commissioned into the 10th Princess Mary's Own Gurkha Rifles before transferring to the Royal Green Jackets. During his first tour in Northern Ireland in 1971 he earned the Military Cross and five years later was promoted to lieutenant colonel and given command of the 2nd Battalion which, in December 1977, was deployed to South Armagh for a two-year resident tour.

South Armagh. Bandit Country. Throughout the long years of 'the Troubles' this was the most dangerous part of Northern Ireland for the British Army. For the Green Jackets, the tour was already proving to be an eventful one. Within weeks of their arrival, PIRA had launched a mortar attack on the joint RUC/Army base in the village of Forkhill where they were stationed, injuring several soldiers. The flatbed lorry from which the mortars were fired was soon found by the soldiers and checked out by an ATO, who declared it free of booby traps. But, as two RUC officers started up the lorry, intending to drive it to another police station for forensic examination, the cab exploded. Missed by the ATO during his examination was a small explosive device, hidden inside the windscreen washer bottle.

Corden-Lloyd helped pull the injured policemen clear of the burning wreckage and both went on to make full recoveries. Fortunately, nobody had been killed in the double attack, but the incident served as a stark reminder of the cunning and ruthless nature of the enemy the men of the Royal Green Jackets were up against in South Armagh.

The archetypal soldier's soldier, Corden-Lloyd was highly respected by his men. Andy McNab, the SAS soldier turned bestselling author, who served under Corden-Lloyd in South Armagh, called him 'the best officer I'd ever met', and he was known to his men as a commander who led from the front.

So when on the afternoon of 17 February 1978 a radio call came into the Operations Room at Bessbrook Mill, the Army's main base in South Armagh, reporting a major contact between one of his units and PIRA gunmen near the border village of Jonesborough, Corden-Lloyd didn't hesitate. He immediately jumped into a Gazelle with his battalion adjutant, Captain Schofield, and ordered the pilot, Sergeant Ives, to fly him to the scene of the firefight.

The contact report was radioed in by a member of the Green Jackets' Close Observation Platoon, or COP. These were units made up of the best men in each infantry battalion, whose job, as the name suggests, was to gather intelligence by conducting covert surveillance of terrorist suspects at close quarters, often remaining in position for days at a time.

The Green Jackets' COP was dug into concealed positions at the southern end of Jonesborough, overlooking the Edenappa Road leading into the staunchly republican village, where intelligence indicated PIRA were planning to set up an IVCP.

After hours of waiting, it was beginning to look as if the terrorists were not going to appear. Then, at around 1620 hours, the calm of the late afternoon was suddenly shattered by the rattle of automatic gunfire, as one of the COP team's positions came under attack from gunmen hidden behind a stone wall a short distance away. Once again, PIRA's South Armagh brigade had demonstrated its skill at uncovering a covert observation post in its midst.

The firefight between the Green Jackets and PIRA was still raging when Corden-Lloyd's Gazelle arrived at the scene less than ten minutes later, accompanied by a Scout helicopter carrying the Airborne Reaction Force, consisting of a medic and three men of the 2nd Bn Light Infantry.

Unable to pinpoint the firing positions of the terrorists on the first low pass over the area, Corden-Lloyd ordered Sergeant Ives to make another pass. As he did so, a stream of 7.62mm tracer rounds flashed by the Gazelle as a PIRA volunteer armed with a belt-fed M60 machine gun turned his attention to the helicopter. Ives reacted instinctively, pulling up and banking hard to the left in a desperate attempt to evade the incoming fire.

The COP soldiers and those onboard the Scout watched in horror as the helicopter then appeared to lose power and plummeted downwards, hitting the ground and briefly rising up into the air again before crashing back down for a second and final time, its spinning rotor blades thrashing into the earth as it cartwheeled across a field. Finally, the helicopter came to rest on its side 100 metres away from the initial point of impact, a crumpled wreck.

Time seemed to stand still for a few seconds. Then, the four men of the ARF hover-jumped from the Scout and raced over to the crash site, under fire from the terrorist gunmen. Moments later two words crackled over the COP unit's radio, bringing a stunned silence to the men: 'Sunray down!' Dave Pomfrett, one of the COP soldiers, remembered the moment well. 'We looked around for someone to make sense of it,' he recalled. 'However, we all knew what it meant.'

Lieutenant Colonel Ian Corden-Lloyd had just become the most senior British officer to be killed on active duty in Northern Ireland.

Introduction

Amid little fanfare, at midnight on 31 July 2007 Operation BANNER, the British Army's codename for its involvement in Northern Ireland during the period commonly referred to as the 'Troubles', officially came to an end. What began as a limited deployment, intended to last only a few weeks to separate nationalist and loyalist mobs after an outbreak of fierce sectarian rioting in the summer of 1969, became the longest continuous military campaign in the history of the British Army.

Initially deployed in a strictly peacekeeping capacity, within months the Army's role changed to one of counter-terrorism as soldiers increasingly came under attack from terrorist groups, chief among them being the Provisional IRA. For the next three decades the military, along with the RUC, was engaged in countering a savage urban and rural insurgency, in which thousands were killed and injured, until the signing of the Belfast Agreement in April 1998 finally brought the prospect of a lasting peace to the war-weary country.

The conflict in Northern Ireland has often been called a 'corporals' war', for it was the junior NCOs leading their 'bricks' on patrol day in, day out on the dangerous streets of Belfast and Londonderry, and in the deceptively tranquil countryside of the border areas, who were at the forefront of the conflict.

But, like Vietnam, Northern Ireland was also a helicopter war. Throughout the long years of Operation BANNER, helicopter crews of the Army Air Corps, Royal Navy and Royal Air Force flew in support of the thousands of security forces personnel serving in the province. They sustained isolated bases in the border areas, evacuated casualties, carried out aerial surveillance, patrolled the waters in and around Northern Ireland and even, towards the end of the conflict, served in a limited offensive capacity.

And nowhere was the air war in Northern Ireland more intense than in South Armagh, an area that became known as Bandit Country, due to its long history of lawlessness and to the strength of the IRA there. If the helicopter was a valuable tool in other parts of Northern Ireland, in South Armagh it was absolutely essential.

From the mid-1970s the danger posed by roadside IEDs to the security forces' mobile patrols in South Armagh forced soldiers off the roads and into the air. By the 1980s Bessbrook Mill, the Army's main base in County Armagh, had become the busiest heliport in Europe, with an average of 600 flights in and out of the base per week.

In the observation role helicopters also became a vital element of the Army's counter-terrorism strategy. Along with fixed-wing types like the de Havilland-Canada Beaver and Britten-Norman Islander, helicopters fitted with increasingly sophisticated surveillance equipment played a key role in many of the security forces' operations, leading to the capture of suspects and forcing the terrorist groups to abandon many of their attacks. Small wonder that the IRA soon came to fear and loathe the helicopter, one volunteer in their East Tyrone brigade stating in his memoirs that he dreamed of watching them 'fall out of the sky in flames'.

Turning that dream into reality became an overriding preoccupation of PIRA's feared South Armagh brigade. Regarded by the security forces as the most skilled and disciplined of PIRA's units, they were not slow in recognizing just how dangerously dependent the British Army had become on helicopters in South Armagh, and set about trying to exploit that vulnerability, with rotary-wing aircraft becoming one of their prime military targets from the mid-1970s onwards.

Only in the skies over South Armagh, PIRA believed, could an outright strategic victory over their enemy be achieved. If they could make the skies as dangerous for the security forces as they had the roads, the British Army would be effectively paralyzed. 'We felt that if we could nullify the helicopter, we would be well on the way to winning the war,' said one volunteer.[1]

The British Army itself concurred with that assessment. The Army's official report analyzing military operations in Northern Ireland during

Operation BANNER, published in 2006, stated: 'Any loss of control of the air would have seriously impeded the conduct of security force operations on the ground'.[2]

Besides the purely military value of downing helicopters, there was also a secondary – and perhaps equally important – aim for PIRA in carrying out attacks on helicopters. As one of the world's most media-savvy militant nationalist movements, the Provisional IRA was well aware of the immense propaganda value to be gained from shooting down military aircraft. The Provisionals were keen to portray themselves as a legitimate guerrilla army, engaged in an armed struggle against what they characterized as a force of colonial occupation. Attacking high-profile military targets like helicopters not only guaranteed PIRA widespread media coverage but also fitted in perfectly with the image they wished to convey of themselves as heroic freedom fighters to their supporters, both at home and abroad.

This explains why the organization went to such lengths during the three decades of the 'Troubles' to bring down helicopters. From taking pot-shots with Tommy guns and Garand rifles in the early years of the conflict to meticulously planned ambushes by large active service units of a dozen or more volunteers, armed with rocket-propelled grenade launchers and 12.7mm heavy machine guns, their determination to shoot down British military aircraft became an obsession, one that would lead PIRA to embark on an international arms hunt spanning more than a decade to procure the one weapon they were convinced could tip the balance of the war in South Armagh in their favour: the heat-seeking surface-to-air missile launcher.

Despite all that effort, their 'kills' were few. The Provisional IRA never did succeed in turning South Armagh into another Vietnam, as they hoped; the loss of Lieutenant Colonel Corden-Lloyd's Gazelle in February 1978 was one of just six helicopters brought down, either directly or indirectly, by hostile fire during the 'Troubles'.

But the figures alone do not tell the whole story, for as this book reveals there were many other attacks which came terrifyingly close to success. That PIRA ultimately failed in its stated goal to halt movement by air in

South Armagh, as well as the other border regions where guerrilla activity was also intense, was due in large part to the skill and professionalism of the Army, Royal Navy and RAF crews.

What follows in these pages is the untold story of that air war between the years 1969 and 2007 when the Provisional IRA and the British security forces fought their long, gruelling battle for control of the skies over Bandit Country.

Chapter One

Troubled Times

ircraft were first used to help combat the IRA during the conflict known to the British as the Anglo-Irish War and to the Irish
as the War of Independence, which broke out in January 1919
when Irish republican irregulars – usually referred to at the time by
the British as Sinn Féiners, or simply 'Shinners' – launched an armed
insurrection.

For the next two and a half years the IRA, under the leadership of
their charismatic commander, Michael Collins, waged a skilful guerrilla campaign against the Crown forces on the island, particularly in the
south-west of the country. Eventually, the Army was forced to garrison
Ireland with over 40,000 troops to support the increasingly beleaguered
Royal Irish Constabulary, which bore the brunt of IRA attacks, and even
this force was deemed insufficient to defeat the insurgency.

Though primarily a ground war, fought between lightly-armed insurgents, employing classic hit-and-run tactics, and a conventional army
more accustomed to fighting a clearly identifiable enemy on the battlefield, airpower provided by the recently formed Royal Air Force would
also play a significant part in the conflict.

The RAF's contribution initially comprised Nos. 105 and 106
Squadrons, both equipped with Bristol F2B fighters serving in the army
co-operation role and based at Omagh in County Tyrone and Fermoy in
County Cork, with further Bristols and Airco DH9s arriving as the war
intensified, and dispersed to aerodromes at Baldonnel and Tallaght near
Dublin, Oranmore in County Galway, Castlebar in County Mayo and
Aldergrove near Belfast.

By 1920 the RAF force in Ireland amounted to around thirty-six aircraft, though the poor serviceability that plagued the squadrons often
reduced the operational force to around half this number.[1]

Armed with two to three machine guns and capable of carrying 110kg of bombs, the Bristol Fighter, or 'Brisfit' as it was nicknamed, was one of the finest two-seater combat aircraft of the First World War, and afterwards saw extensive service in the 'aerial policing' role the RAF undertook in restive parts of the Empire.

For veterans of the air war over the Western Front, like Australian Flying Officer F.C. Penny, hunting elusive, fleet-footed irregulars across rural Ireland was to prove a frustrating task. 'With our Bristol fighters we searched the mountain sides and glens but rarely found anything of significance to report,' he admitted.[2]

Even when the crews did chance upon what they believed to be IRA men, a ban on using weapons from aircraft in Ireland imposed by a British government nervous of civilian casualties meant that they were unable to take direct action against the enemy themselves.

The Lord Lieutenant of Ireland, Sir John French, pressed for the RAF to be used in a more offensive capacity. In this he was joined by the GOC Ireland, General Sir Nevil Macready, who argued that there were 'undoubtedly cases where fire from aeroplanes would materially assist the forces on the ground, with little or no danger to harmless individuals'.

Air Marshal Sir Hugh 'Boom' Trenchard, the redoubtable chief of the Royal Air Force, begged to differ. Opposing French and Macready's calls for the use of armed aircraft in Ireland, Trenchard argued that 'reckless use of such a powerful arm, which once loosed in the air cannot be delicately controlled, will…engender great bitterness', and warned that 'a great popular outcry will be created against the unfortunate pilots who are involved in the action, from which it will be impossible to shield them'.[3]

Winston Churchill, the Secretary of State for War, was more sympathetic to French and Macready's request, believing that armed aircraft could provide 'a great deterrent to illegal drilling and rebel gatherings'. On 1 July 1920 he wrote: 'I see no objection from a military point of view … to aeroplanes being dispatched with definite orders in each particular case to disperse them by machine-gun fire or bombs, using of course no more force than is necessary to scatter and stampede them.'[4] But his was a lone voice in Prime Minister Lloyd George's Cabinet and for the time being Trenchard's view prevailed.

Perhaps ignorant of the restrictions imposed by Trenchard and the government, the RAF's contribution came in for strong criticism from some Army officers. Writing in 1923, the future hero of El Alamein, Bernard Law Montgomery, who during the latter stages of the Anglo-Irish War served as a major with 17 Infantry Brigade, stationed in Cork, stated bluntly:

> [Aeroplanes] were really of no use to us, except as a quick and safe means of getting from one place to another. Even then the landing grounds were few and far between. The pilots and observers knew nothing whatever about the war, or the conditions under which it was being fought, and were not therefore in a position to be able to help much.[5]

The IRA, however, had a healthy respect for British airpower and would often break off an ambush if an aircraft was spotted overhead. IRA Commandant Matthew Barry recalled how he and his men were relentlessly harassed by an RAF fighter while fleeing across the County Kildare countryside, following an aborted attack on a troop train at the town of Celbridge, near Dublin: 'The plane several times swooped down on us and on one occasion we had to throw ourselves flat on the ground to avoid being rammed by it. Even then, it almost touched the ground.'[6]

Prevented from playing a more active part in the fighting, the crews of the RAF's F2Bs and DH9s instead found employment carrying out observation work, transporting senior officers and providing an air mail service to isolated garrisons in the south-west of the country, where frequent IRA ambushes made travel on the narrow country lanes a hazardous business. The blocking of roads by the rebels, either through trenching or using felled trees, and the discovery that the IRA were tapping telegraph lines also forced commanders to increasingly rely on the RAF to convey despatches between bases.

This held its own dangers, however. In May 1921 a Bristol suffering engine trouble made a forced landing in a field in County Limerick, an IRA stronghold. When a local IRA unit arrived on the scene they found the two crewmen trying to destroy the documents they were carrying. Unfortunately they didn't succeed and the top secret papers fell into enemy hands.

The IRA also began to specifically target British aircraft. Early on the morning of 14 August 1920 an IRA unit tried to destroy a Bristol that force-landed near Banteer, County Cork, after being hit by rifle fire. One of the soldiers guarding the stricken Bristol was killed in the IRA's follow-up attack, though according to a statement issued by the British Army's Irish Command: 'The remainder of the guard immediately engaged their opponents and put them to flight.'[7]

Two weeks later the IRA met with greater success after another Bristol made an emergency landing between Fermoy and Lismore, this time due to mechanical failure. A group of 'Shinners' attacked the crew and then destroyed the aeroplane. A further Bristol was destroyed on the ground and its observer, Flying Officer MacKay, taken prisoner by an IRA flying column after coming down at Kilfinnane, County Limerick, on 11 February 1921. The captured airman and his IRA guards apparently got on well, and he was later released unharmed. 'We found our prisoner a very likeable person, fairly well educated for an Englishman, and felt rather sorry at his departure,' said one of his captors.[8]

Meanwhile, on the ground the war escalated. The Royal Irish Constabulary began to crumble under the sustained pressure of IRA attacks and the British government responded by forming the Royal Irish Constabulary Special Reserve (RICSR), a force of temporary constables recruited from the ranks of ex-soldiers, and the Auxiliary Division, known as 'Auxies', made up of former Army officers. The RICSR became better known as the 'Black and Tans', but this nickname was also commonly applied to the Auxiliaries, who gained a reputation for brutality.

Growing frustration at the effective hit-and-run tactics employed by Collins's men led to renewed calls from Macready for armed air support from the RAF, which the Army believed could restrict the freedom of movement the IRA enjoyed. In March 1921 the government finally lifted its ban on the use of armament on aircraft. But crews were to be governed by tight rules of engagement. They were prohibited from flying over heavily populated areas and were to fire only on insurgents who could be positively identified as such – and then only when they were actually engaging Crown forces or had just done so.

But by this stage in the war a few armed patrols made little difference. Recognizing that there was no military solution to the situation, Lloyd George was already moving towards a negotiated settlement with the Sinn Fein leadership and by the time a truce was declared between the two sides in July 1921 only a small number of armed sorties had been carried out by the RAF.

Negotiations led to the signing of a treaty by the British government and Michael Collins in December, granting independence to southern Ireland, which would be known as the Irish Free State. The north-eastern six counties that made up the bulk of the historic province of Ulster, however, would remain part of the United Kingdom, as per the wishes of its unionist majority.

But hopes that this agreement would bring an end to the bloodshed proved optimistic. The Anglo-Irish Treaty failed to satisfy hardliners in the IRA, who viewed the partition of Ireland as a betrayal of republican ideals and vowed to continue an armed struggle aimed at achieving full independence for a unified Ireland.

Civil war was now inevitable, and broke out in June 1922, fought between anti-Treaty elements of the IRA and the forces of the Provisional Government of the new Irish Free State, led by Collins. As the two sides turned on each other, the RAF quietly withdrew from its bases in southern Ireland.

With Collins declining an offer from Churchill to use RAF crews and aircraft with Free State markings to bomb the Four Courts building in Dublin, where a large number of IRA volunteers were holed up, the task of fighting the anti-Treaty forces from the air fell to the newly constituted Irish National Army Air Service, equipped with a handful of ex-RAF machines. In May 1923 the brief but bitter Irish Civil War ended with the anti-Treaty IRA defeated, the war's most high profile casualty being Collins, killed in an ambush by irregulars in County Cork on 22 August 1922.

Operation HARVEST

Another thirty-five years would pass before British airmen were once again called upon to help fight Irish insurgents.

After the Second World War the IRA was widely regarded as a spent force, riven by internal divisions and discredited by its wartime involvement with the Nazis. But in the first half of the 1950s the organization was secretly building itself up for a renewed armed offensive, though this time it would be confined to the border areas of Ulster. Raids on armouries in England and Northern Ireland were carried out, the largest taking place at Gough Barracks in County Armagh in June 1954, netting the organization hundreds of Lee-Enfield rifles and Sten guns, while a new generation of young recruits underwent training in guerrilla warfare in the countryside of southern Ireland.

In December 1956 the IRA leadership finally felt ready to confront the Royal Ulster Constabulary and British Army units stationed in Northern Ireland. For the IRA, it must've seemed a propitious time to launch an insurrection, with the British Lion licking its wounds after the Suez debacle the previous month, which saw the country's international prestige sink to an all-time low, and British forces heavily committed fighting insurgents in Malaya and Cyprus.

The Border campaign, or Operation HARVEST as it was named by the IRA's chief strategist, Sean Cronin, opened on the night of 12 December with a series of co-ordinated attacks on police stations, Army barracks and customs posts by an estimated force of 150 IRA volunteers. Initially taken by surprise, the Northern Ireland government at Stormont responded swiftly by introducing internment on 21 December. A few days later RUC Constable John Scally became the first fatality of the campaign when he was shot whilst fending off an IRA attack on his police station in County Fermanagh.

Airpower was brought to bear in the campaign against the IRA in February 1957 with the arrival of five Auster AOP.6 spotter planes of

1913 Light Liaison Flight (which became 13 Flight, 651 Squadron, upon the formation of the Army Air Corps in September) at RAF Aldergrove, under the command of Captain Peter Wilson, who had earned a DFC in the Korean War.

Originally serving in the artillery-spotting role during the Second World War, the Auster found a new niche for itself as Britain's primary airborne counter-insurgency platform in post-war colonial trouble spots, carrying out visual and photographic reconnaissance, communications, leaflet-dropping and target-marking duties.

In Northern Ireland, the Austers' main job was to carry out observation patrols along the border and assist the RUC in searches for IRA men following attacks. A typical search by Austers, carried out on 7 September 1958, resulted in the capture of two suspects after an Orange Hall was blown up in County Fermanagh.[9]

Unable to sustain the momentum of attacks carried out in the initial phase of the campaign, IRA activity slackened during the second half of 1957, with the introduction of internment south of the border in July proving a major blow, denying the guerrillas a safe haven in the Irish Republic.

By March 1959 IRA activity had dwindled to a point where Dublin felt confident enough to end internment (though it was maintained by Stormont for a further two years). This turned out to be a premature move, for a few months later the IRA relaunched its campaign with a series of shootings and bombings. In response, the air assets available to support the RUC were supplemented with the arrival of several helicopters, firstly, in September 1959, four Bristol Sycamores of 118 Squadron, followed by three Army Air Corps Saunders-Roe Skeeters in February 1960.

The latter was a basic, underpowered but highly agile machine, the AAC's first operational helicopter, whose lack of capability in 'hot and high' conditions confined it to the cooler climes of northern Europe. Sergeant Major Martin Forde, who flew the Skeeter in Northern Ireland in the 1960s, said of it:

> You could hardly lift it with two people in and fuel . .... Once you
> got it into the air it was a dream to fly. But most people didn't

like it because it was difficult to get off the ground. You had to do a running take-off sometimes, in summer especially.[10]

Despite the limited capabilities of early helicopters like the Sycamore, in the campaigns against communist insurgents in Malaya and the nationalist guerrillas of EOKA in Cyprus they proved invaluable. Field Marshal Lord Harding, Governor of Cyprus during the Emergency there, credited the RAF's Sycamore-equipped 284 Squadron with having 'contributed more to fighting terrorism on the island than any other single unit'.[11]

It wasn't just the British who were beginning to appreciate the importance of the helicopter in Internal Security operations. A manual written by IRA strategist Sean Cronin setting out tactics for Operation HARVEST specifically advised volunteers to be on the alert for helicopters:

> Enemy increasingly uses helicopters against guerrillas. Guerrillas on the move must always be on the watch for enemy aircraft. One of the best protections is a standard warning system .... Air guards should watch for aircraft when in camp. The drill is – scatter, hit the ground, take cover.[12]

Cronin was right to fear the helicopter. Though small in number, the Sycamores in particular soon proved their worth, offering the security forces great tactical flexibility through rapid insertion of troops or RUC officers to the scene of an incident, often cutting off the retreat of fleeing IRA volunteers.

The RUC came to rely heavily on their new mode of transport. On 25 August 1960 Albert Kennedy, the Deputy Inspector-General of the RUC, wrote that the Sycamores 'had proved of inestimable value to the Royal Ulster Constabulary in anti IRA operations',[13] while Squadron Leader David Toon, 118 OC, noted that 'the Royal Ulster Constabulary emphasize the deterrent value of the presence of helicopters in their support'.[14]

Attacks plummeted from a high of 341 in 1957 to a mere twenty-six in 1960. Among that handful, however, one was particularly significant, being the first recorded occasion in which the IRA attacked a helicopter.

On 2 February 1960 three Sycamores were involved in a major cordon and search operation near Tullyrossmearan in County Fermanagh when, as it came in to land RUC officers, one of the helicopters was fired on by IRA gunmen armed with Thompson sub-machine guns. No hits were registered and the suspects were later captured by Gardaí after fleeing across the border. 'On being questioned they confirmed they had fired at the helicopter,' recorded 118's ORB. This attack was proof, Toon wrote, of the IRA's 'displeasure at the use of helicopters'.[15]

The failure to bring down the Sycamore reflected the wider failure of Operation HARVEST. The campaign limped on for another two years, until even the hardliners were forced to confront the fact that the Border campaign had failed. On 26 February 1962 the IRA issued a statement declaring a cessation of hostilities, though ominously it went on to warn that the organization 'looks forward with confidence ... to a period of consolidation, expansion and preparation for the final and victorious phase of the struggle for the full freedom of Ireland'.

Casualties during the Border campaign had been light: six police-men and ten IRA members and their helpers killed (five in an 'own goal' explosion). The Army Air Corps lost two Austers in accidents, claiming the lives of three airmen, while the RAF lost a single Sycamore, again in an accident.[16]

In August 1962 118 Squadron was disbanded. Its last OC, Squadron Leader Francis Hart, wrote in his operational diary: 'Operationally quiet. No news of IRA activity of note. It seems very unlikely that trouble will re-open for some considerable time – if ever!'[17]

How misplaced was that optimism would become apparent seven years later when another, far more savage and much more protracted, conflict would engulf Northern Ireland.

Raising the Banner

When the 'Troubles', as the violence that ravaged Northern Ireland became known, exploded in the summer of 1969, following months of growing sectarian tension between the unionist and nationalist communities, military air assets stationed in the province consisted of six Sioux of the 17th/21st Lancers Air Squadron and four more of the Prince of Wales's Own Regiment of Yorkshire, based at RAF Aldergrove and Ballykelly in County Londonderry.

Known as the 'Clockwork Mouse', the Westland Sioux was a licence-built version of the American Bell 47G, a helicopter that gained fame for its casualty evacuation (casevac) role during the Korean War. Well-liked by its pilots, it was, however, slow and had very limited carrying capacity, though its distinctive bubble canopy offered unimpaired visibility, making it ideal for airborne surveillance – the main task it would perform in Northern Ireland.

The Sioux were joined by a detachment of three Wessex helicopters of the RAF's 72 Squadron, based at Odiham, which flew out to Ballykelly in July before relocating to RAF Aldergrove soon after to enhance the air mobility of the RUC and Northern Ireland's peacetime garrison of around 2,500 troops.

At this stage, however, the British government was anxious to avoid an overt military involvement in what was still seen as a purely law and order problem, to be handled by the RUC. Consequently, a request by the police for helicopters to be employed in aerial surveillance of demonstrations was initially turned down. 'In the case of direct overhead surveillance of a crowd, the involvement of British military personnel would be so direct, and the risk of inflaming an already tense situation would be so great, that I consider this [request] clearly unacceptable,' Minister of Defence for Administration Roy Hattersley wrote in a July 1969 memo.[18]

But events on the ground were fast gaining a momentum of their own. Any lingering hopes that the RUC alone would be able to contain the escalating inter-communal violence ended in August, when several days and nights of brutal rioting in Londonderry and Belfast left ten dead, hundreds injured and thousands of people displaced, driven out of their homes by loyalist and nationalist mobs.

With the RUC exhausted and discredited in the eyes of many Catholics, on 14 August the government ordered British troops – a company from the 1st Bn Prince of Wales's Own Regiment of Yorkshire, which was already stationed in the province – onto the streets of Londonderry to restore order. The next day more soldiers arrived from England, marking the beginning of Operation BANNER.

By the end of August troop numbers in Northern Ireland had swollen to 6,000. As more and more soldiers poured into the province, the modest helicopter force was expanded to meet the increasing demands placed upon it. On 17 August the Wessex force based at Aldergrove was increased to seven, becoming the RAF's Support Helicopter Detachment Northern Ireland. A day later 8 Flight Army Air Corps arrived, equipped with the sturdy Westland Scout. To co-ordinate the mounting requests for helicopter support, an air tasking cell was established at Aldergrove.

Soon the helicopter force in Northern Ireland would number almost fifty, spread between bases at Bessbrook, County Armagh; Ballykelly, County Londonderry; Omagh, County Tyrone; Long Kesh, County Down and Aldergrove, County Antrim.

The government gave way over aerial surveillance and the Sioux helicopter quickly became a familiar sight over Londonderry and Belfast during riots, helping the troops on the ground identify those orchestrating the trouble and moving in units to deal with them.

Initially British soldiers were warmly welcomed by the majority of the population, both Catholic and Protestant, who were relieved that the Army had managed to bring some stability to the province. In nationalist enclaves of Belfast, like the Ardoyne and Short Strand – places which in the years ahead would become notorious IRA strongholds – British troops were greeted with cups of tea and scones.

But the honeymoon period was to be relatively short-lived. Within a few months relations between the Army and the Catholic community began to break down. The protectors of 1969 came to be regarded by 1971 as a force of occupation, as the Army imposed curfews and carried out heavy-handed house searches in nationalist neighbourhoods looking for arms. This breakdown in community relations was a gift to the Provisional IRA, who exploited the situation to the full.

The Provisionals – or 'Provos' as they became known – came about as a result of a split in the IRA's ranks at the end of 1969, the members of this new breakaway faction being committed to waging an all-out guerrilla campaign against the security forces, just as their predecessors had done in the Anglo-Irish War half a century earlier.

And nowhere would the Provisional IRA prosecute its war more vigorously than in South Armagh, a region of Northern Ireland soon to become better known by another name.

Chapter Two

Bandit Country
aka
'The Independent Republic of South Armagh'

In April 1980 a report landed on the desk of Prime Minister Margaret Thatcher. The report was part of a wide-ranging review of the Intelligence effort against terrorism in Northern Ireland, conducted by the former head of MI6, Sir Maurice Oldfield, which the PM had ordered in the wake of two of the IRA's most devastating and high-profile attacks, the assassination of the Queen's cousin Lord Louis Mountbatten and the massacre of eighteen British soldiers in a bombing at Warrenpoint in County Down, which took place within hours of each other on 27 August 1979.

While observing that, these two attacks notwithstanding, the security situation in most parts of Northern Ireland was steadily improving, when it came to evaluating the situation in South Armagh the report took on a more pessimistic tone. Noting that republican sentiment was deep-rooted, it pointed out that the area 'has a long tradition of lawlessness and violence' where 'the forces of law and order have never had an easy task'. The security forces, it went on, faced 'a small but experienced and determined terrorist threat'. The best chance of countering this threat, the author judged, lay in trying to 'alienate the terrorists from the community.' However, the report gloomily conceded that 'achievement of this goal is a long way off.'[1]

But just how did this small, thinly populated patch of Northern Ireland come to be so troublesome to the British?

Nestling between Tyrone and Down, County Armagh is the smallest of the six counties that make up Northern Ireland, its land mass amounting to 1,326 square kilometres. Though no official boundary line exists, the town of Keady is generally accepted as marking the point at which North Armagh ends and South Armagh begins. Finishing at the border it shares with Counties Monaghan and Louth in the Irish Republic, South Armagh boasts some of the most spectacular scenery in Ireland – a place of rolling hills, farmland, woods and small villages, dominated by the imposing mass of Slieve Gullion (which translates as 'mountain of the steep slope'), an extinct volcano in the south-east of the county and, at 573 metres, its highest peak. But South Armagh's bucolic beauty masks a dark and turbulent history, steeped in a tradition of violent rebellion.

South Armagh became a bastion of Irish Catholic resistance to the English Crown after the Plantation of Ulster in the early seventeenth century, when large numbers of Scots Presbyterian and English Protestant settlers arrived in North Armagh, driving the dispossessed native Irish into the southern portion of the county. But this scheme by King James I to subdue rebellion in Ireland by settling the country with loyal Protestant subjects only led to further unrest, and an uprising broke out in Ulster in 1641, with some of the worst violence occurring in County Armagh, where an estimated 1,250 Protestants were killed.

Over the next three centuries South Armagh would continue to figure prominently in the many bloody conflicts and rebellions that blighted Ireland, and its reputation for lawlessness became well entrenched. Yet despite its Catholic majority and staunchly nationalist character, when the border separating Northern Ireland from the newly established Irish Free State was drawn up following the Anglo-Irish War, South Armagh was included within the territory of Northern Ireland, a situation welcomed neither by unionists nor the majority of its inhabitants. For the people of South Armagh, their forced inclusion in the new state of Northern Ireland was seen as just another in a long line of injustices they'd suffered at the hands of the British.

This ingrained sense of grievance, together with a tradition of violent resistance to authority, would prove an incendiary mix when the political and sectarian tensions that continued to build and fester after partition erupted in 1969 and it wasn't long before the IRA's South Armagh brigade emerged as the British Army's most dangerous opponent.

The 'bandits'

On 11 August 1970 RUC Constables Sam Donaldson and Robert Millar were fatally injured by a booby-trap bomb whilst examining an abandoned car near the town of Crossmaglen, becoming the first members of the security forces to be killed by the Provisional IRA during the 'Troubles'. The attack had been carried out by PIRA's South Armagh brigade, which would rapidly earn itself a reputation for ruthless efficiency.

The fiercely independent character of South Armagh was reflected by the brigade itself which, unlike PIRA's other units, was largely autonomous, financing itself through cross-border smuggling and taking little direction from the Provisional IRA leadership in Belfast. 'In South Armagh they do their own thing ... they run their own war down there,' explained one Provo.[2]

Volunteers drawn from the area had a reputation for being amongst the most hardline. During the 1922-23 Irish Civil War, it was said that all South Armagh IRA men fought on the anti-Treaty side against Michael Collins's Free State forces. Seventy-five years later it was veterans of the South Armagh brigade who went on to form the nucleus of the breakaway Real IRA, which opposed the Northern Ireland peace process.

Many of the British soldiers and RUC officers stationed in South Armagh during the 'Troubles' had a grudging professional respect for the IRA who operated there. A member of the Bessbrook Support Unit, a covert surveillance branch of the RUC active in South Armagh in the late 1970s, commented: 'If I wanted to recruit an army, I could do worse than start with them.'[3]

A British Army assessment from 1974 rated the brigade highly, noting that all their attacks were carefully planned, with escape routes always worked out in advance. In 1975 an anonymous SAS officer offered the following analysis of the South Armagh brigade: 'Well equipped, they are highly professional men, extremely ruthless, and have much experience behind them.' He went on: 'Their success in sophisticated mining and booby-trapping techniques is well known, their shooting is often accurate, and they are even capable of jamming vital communications.'[4]

Though less frequent than those in Northern Ireland's two main cities, Belfast and Londonderry, attacks in South Armagh tended to be on a greater scale, the much reduced risk of inflicting collateral damage among their supporters in this thinly populated rural area meaning the Provisionals could use much larger bombs and unleash more firepower.

For both soldiers and aircrew, South Armagh soon came to acquire a fearsome reputation and all knew that to let your guard down could prove fatal. 'There was always that sense of threat,' said Rear Admiral Chris Parry, who as a lieutenant served as a Wessex observer in Northern Ireland in the 1980s.[5] Aircrew became adept at recognizing the clues that suggested an attack was imminent – no animals in the fields or windows of houses left open, even on a cold day (to prevent the glass being shattered by a bomb explosion) were sure signs of an impending attack.

Despite its name, the South Armagh brigade was a relatively small outfit, with no more than fifty active members at its peak. An RUC Special Branch officer stationed in County Armagh in the 1980s revealed that it was believed the South Armagh IRA comprised three units, each numbering around fifteen volunteers, based in the village of Silverbridge, the border town of Dundalk in County Louth, and in Crossmaglen, which was home to the most senior and experienced members.[6]

Known to the military by the abbreviation XMG and to the locals simply as 'Cross', this small town of around 1,500 inhabitants, lying less than two miles from the border with the Irish Republic, was the centre of IRA activity in South Armagh. Soldiers were surprised at how small this notorious IRA stronghold was upon first arriving there. But more attacks took place in and around this little town than anywhere else in the county, with the heavily fortified joint Army/RUC base in the centre of Crossmaglen often likened to a besieged outpost in enemy territory, attracting regular mortar, machine-gun and sniper attack.

Its notoriety long predated the most recent Troubles. In 1852 the Deputy Inspector General of the Irish Constabulary declared

Crossmaglen to be 'probably the worst part of the country'.[7] A defining episode in its history was the Crossmaglen Conspiracy, in which twelve local men were convicted in 1883 of being members of a group known as the Irish Patriotic Brotherhood, which, in the words of the trial judge, Justice Lawson, was dedicated to the 'overthrow of English rule in this country', and given heavy prison sentences. At the time and ever since the men were seen by local people as victims of a major miscarriage of justice perpetrated by the British State.

In such a strongly republican area, where hostility to the British was so firmly entrenched, winning hearts and minds was never a viable option for the Army, and those who did not support the Provisionals were usually too fearful of reprisals to co-operate with the security forces.

But prosecuting a vigorous counter-terrorism campaign in South Armagh was no easy task, either. The close-knit nature of the community meant that of all the IRA's units, the South Armagh brigade was the least vulnerable to penetration by informers. This, together with their high standard of professionalism, ensured they suffered the fewest losses during the conflict, with only two volunteers killed in action by the security forces up to 1975, even if one of these, Cullyhanna man Michael McVerry – shot whilst planting a bomb at an RUC station in Keady in 1973 – had been one of the brigade's senior commanders.

This lack of success dismayed more offensively minded soldiers, like the anonymous SAS officer quoted above: '...the number of "kills" [by the security forces] are insignificant compared to Army casualty figures,' he admitted. 'It would be surprising if there had been any other terrorist campaigns in which the disparity of the casualty figures have been as great as this.'[8]

Besides the rural environment and support they enjoyed amongst the local population, perhaps the greatest advantage the South Armagh brigade enjoyed over the British Army was the county's border with the Republic. Extending over seventy kilometres, it offered attackers an easy escape into what the British regarded as the relative sanctuary of the Irish Republic – which was strictly off limits to the British security forces – as an NIO memo observed: 'The border, honeycombed by many crossings, offers an opportunity for terrorists to flit to and fro. Many attacks on the security forces have, in the past, been launched from firing positions south of the border.'[9]

From the beginning of the 'Troubles' the British were highly sceptical of Dublin's resolve to tackle IRA activity on their side of the border, and cross-border co-operation was poor. In the 1970s the Garda refused to deal directly with the British Army, only communicating with the RUC. Even then, co-operation was patchy at best. Many British soldiers and RUC officers believed their Irish counterparts were less than fully committed to combating IRA activity on the Republic side of the border, and the issue bedevilled Anglo-Irish relations throughout much of the 'Troubles'. For their part, the Irish pleaded a lack of resources, not resolve, and resented British accusations that the Republic was a safe haven for terrorists mounting cross-border attacks.

The Provisionals, however, were in no doubt about the Republic's importance as a base of operations and were anxious to avoid antagonizing Dublin at all costs. The Green Book, the IRA's official handbook setting out rules for all its members to abide by, expressly prohibited attacks on the Garda and Irish Army. 'Volunteers are strictly forbidden to take any military action against 26 County forces under any circumstances whatsoever,' it stated, pointing out that the importance of this order in the border areas 'cannot be over-emphasized'.

London's frustration over the poor state of security co-operation along the border was revealed in a 1974 memo from the Secretary of State for Northern Ireland, Merlyn Rees, to the Irish Foreign Minister, Garret FitzGerald: 'It is a great handicap to the security forces in Northern Ireland that terrorists can escape across the border; that they can lay mines and fire across this land frontier.'[10]

While terrorist violence steadily declined throughout most parts of Northern Ireland after reaching its peak in 1972 – a year in which 496 people were killed and the province was rocked by more than 1,300 explosions and 10,000 shootings – in South Armagh the level of terrorist incidents remained constant, and even increased. Highlighting this trend, a government memo of 25 February 1975 assessing the levels of violence during 1974 commented that 'The weakening of the terrorist forces in Belfast and Londonderry and the arrests of many of their leaders forced terrorist activities to be diverted to the rural and border areas.'[11]

By late 1975 terrorist violence in South Armagh was spiralling out of control. Despite PIRA having called a ceasefire at the start of the year, killings in South Armagh continued. MPs were now calling South Armagh a no-go area for the Army. Airey Neave, the Conservatives' Northern Ireland spokesman, talked of there being 'anarchy in South Armagh', which was 'virtually IRA-occupied territory'.[12] Some in the Army admitted as much. 'The Provisionals have declared this area the Independent Republic of South Armagh,' one unnamed British officer told the press at the time, 'and regrettably this assertion is not very far from the truth.'[13]

The violence reached a peak in January 1976, when months of mounting sectarian bloodshed perpetrated by republican and loyalist terrorists culminated in the horrific Kingsmills massacre, in which a minibus carrying workmen from a textiles factory in the South Armagh village of Kingsmills was stopped by a PIRA gang, who forced the Protestant passengers off the minibus and executed ten of them in cold blood.

With the government under intense political pressure, on 12 January 1976 Prime Minister Harold Wilson made a speech to the House of Commons announcing that he had authorized the despatch of the SAS to South Armagh to restore order there. Although the move was seen by some as a mere PR exercise, intended to intimidate the IRA and placate those who had accused the government of being soft on terrorism, the deployment of the British Army's elite special forces unit marked a dramatic escalation of the counter-terrorism effort in Northern Ireland.[14] The regiment's involvement in the Troubles would prove highly controversial, but the SAS also enjoyed considerable success against the terrorists and played a key role in helping to contain terrorism in Northern Ireland.

While Wilson designated South Armagh a 'special emergency area' in his speech, it was the name his Secretary of State for Northern Ireland, Merlyn Rees, had bestowed on the area a few weeks earlier that was seized on by the media. Explaining that South Armagh was 'an unusual area where there is little support for the Security Forces', in a statement issued on 23 November 1975 he called it 'bandit country'.[15] Local people unsurprisingly took exception to the label. 'For 10 years British propaganda has denigrated South Armagh as "bandit country",' said nationalist Armagh politician Seamus Mallon in 1982. 'This is bitterly resented by the people of South Armagh, the vast majority of whom are opposed to violence.'[16] Many British soldiers, however, thought the description apt.

Battle for the roads

During the first half of the 1970s the IRA waged a brutal bombing campaign against the Army's mobile patrols in South Armagh, aimed at forcing the Army off the roads. The few routes leading in and out of bases in South Armagh meant that it was easy for the IRA to predict the movements of patrols and pick off Army vehicles with IEDs – often hidden in culverts – detonated by command-wire, as an MoD memo admitted: 'The opportunities presented to the terrorists by the limited number of approach routes to border bases to use culvert mines to ambush Security Forces vehicles threaten all supply runs and mobile patrols.'[17]

Trooper John Warnock of the Royal Tank Regiment became the first British soldier killed in a roadside bomb attack when the Land Rover he was travelling in was hit on 4 September 1971 near Newry by a seven kilogram device planted by the Official IRA, the Marxist wing of the militant republican movement. The South Armagh brigade joined this campaign on 10 February 1972, when a Land Rover carrying soldiers of the Devonshire and Dorset Regiment was blown twenty feet in the air by a twenty-two kilogram bomb near Cullyhanna, killing two soldiers. Two more soldiers, this time from the 2nd Bn Parachute Regiment, died when their Land Rover was destroyed near Newtownhamilton on 7 April 1973.

With soft-skinned Land Rovers proving far too vulnerable to this kind of attack, the Army turned increasingly to armoured vehicles like the Ferret scout car and the Saracen. The IRA's response was to use larger IEDs.

Two Ferrets were blown up within weeks of each other in July and August 1972, both attacks taking place near Crossmaglen. Nor did the Saracen prove any more resistant to the IRA's bombs. These six-wheeled armoured personnel carriers, known to the troops as 'Sarrycans', were not popular with soldiers, being highly vulnerable to IEDs. That vulnerability was exposed in horrific fashion on 10 September 1972 when a Saracen was ripped apart by a roadside bomb whilst patrolling near Dungannon in County Tyrone, killing three soldiers, injuring five others and leaving a crater twenty feet deep in the road. At over 200kg, this was the largest bomb detonated in Northern Ireland up to that point. On the same day another Saracen had a lucky escape in South Armagh, passing by a bomb hidden in a milk churn in the village of Drumintee just before it went off, and on 3 December 1973 two Saracens were blown across a road in the border village of Killeen, injuring four soldiers.

Finally, after Corporal Edward Gleeson of the 3rd Bn Royal Regiment of Fusiliers was killed and two other soldiers badly wounded when their Saracen was hit by another massive IED hidden in a culvert near Crossmaglen on 9 October 1975, followed by the deaths of three more soldiers in March 1976 when their Land Rover was destroyed as it crossed a bridge at Belleek, Army commanders decided to switch to heliborne patrols.

A so-called 'no-drive line' stretching from Newtownhamilton in the west of the county to Newry in the east was reportedly drawn up, below which vehicle movement by the security forces was effectively banned.[18] With only rare exceptions, wheeled transport was confined to unmarked civilian vehicles, known as 'Q cars', used on covert operations, and when an Operation TONNAGE had to be carried out. These involved the Army virtually closing down Crossmaglen by setting up VCPs on all the approach roads so that a convoy of lorries could safely transport heavy equipment and materials, that couldn't be airlifted, into the base.

Though it made sound tactical sense to use helicopters in South Armagh, the decision to abandon the roads came in for sharp criticism from some politicians, who viewed it as further proof that South Armagh was now under the de facto control of the Provisionals. In January 1976, Conservative MP Sir Nigel Fisher declared in Parliament:

The truth is that for many months, almost years now, the
Queen's writ has ceased to run in the border areas of County
Armagh, which is now Provo Country. The RUC and the Army
can scarcely use the roads for fear of mines or an ambush, and
many of their posts have to be supplied by helicopter. That, in
a part of the United Kingdom, is a disgraceful and humiliating
state of affairs.[19]

Some Army officers agreed. One of them was General Alistair Irwin who,
as a lieutenant colonel in the mid-1980s, commanded the 1st Bn The
Black Watch in South Armagh and went on to become GOC Northern
Ireland. 'This irritated me; that Her Majesty's Forces could not drive
the roads of South Armagh because of the threat of terrorist activity was
monstrous,' he later said. Determined to reassert the Army's authority,
during the battalion's 1985 tour he and his men carried out several days
of road patrols, after careful planning, in defiance of the IRA threat. '…
we went everywhere in vehicles; we temporarily grounded the helicopters for everything except emergencies.' But he was frustrated that his
example was not followed. 'I was disappointed, but not surprised, to discover when I went back as GOC 15 years later that, in terms of tactical
transport in South Armagh, no progress of any kind had been made.'[20]

Chapter Three

'Everything was done by helicopter'

With the roads all but out of bounds to the security forces, the helicopter came to assume immense strategic importance in South Armagh, with the Army almost completely dependent on helicopters to conduct day-to-day operations in the area. 'We were flown everywhere ... we didn't conduct mobile patrols at all,' confirmed one Royal Marine. The insertion and extraction of foot patrols, surveillance, the re-supply of bases, casualty evacuation ... 'Everything,' said Major General Julian Thompson, who commanded 40 Commando Royal Marines in South Armagh in 1976, 'was done by helicopter.'[1]

The busiest heliport in Europe

The centre of helicopter operations in South Armagh was Bessbrook Mill, a linen factory dating from the eighteenth century, around which Quaker John Grubb Richardson built the village of Bessbrook as a home for his workers when he bought the derelict factory in 1845. By the early 1970s the factory was out of business but it found a new lease of life when the British Army, requiring a base for troops and helicopters in South Armagh, requisitioned the Mill.

A cheerless building with bricked-up windows and thus no natural light, it's remembered with little affection by those who were stationed there, one para describing it as a 'real stinking horrible base'. Facilities in the early days were basic. 'The pilots used to land on two elevated piles of railway sleepers on scaffolding,' revealed the para.[2] But soon things began to change, with purpose-built helicopter landing sites and improved troop accommodation. Still, even by the end of the 'Troubles', Lieutenant Commander Andy Hurry – who commanded the last helicopter unit to be based at Bessbrook Mill in 2007, a detachment of Royal Navy Lynx – reckoned it was 'more like a prison than somewhere to base a military force'.[3]

At the height of the 'Troubles' there were around 600 flights in and out of the base each week, with an average of 15,000 personnel being transported per month,[4] making the base the busiest heliport in Europe and earning it the nickname 'Bessbrook International' from locals. Helicopter landing sites were also established in the grounds of the security forces bases in Forkhill, Newtownhamilton and Crossmaglen which along with most other military posts dotted throughout South Armagh, relied almost entirely on helicopters for re-supply, even having their rubbish flown out.

When Operation BANNER commenced, the standard light utility helicopter operated by the Army was the Westland Scout AH1. Though rather small – being able to carry only four troops besides a two-man crew – it was a tough and reliable machine: a 'flying Land Rover', in the words of one pilot. Scouts were often used to carry out 'Eagle' patrols in the border areas, in which the helicopter would swoop down to land the four-man patrol it was carrying to set up snap VCPs in an effort to interdict the cross-border movement of arms and terrorists.

Providing a heavier lift capability were the Wessex of the Support Helicopter Detachment Northern Ireland, supplemented from 1972 with small numbers of Pumas, drawn first from 33 and later from 230 Squadron, whose crews were rotated on six-week 'roulement' tours.

The Westland Wessex HC2, a licence-built version of the US Navy's Sikorsky S-58, entered service in 1963. Powered by two Rolls-Royce Gnome turboshaft engines, it could carry up to sixteen passengers or 1,800kg of cargo and was highly regarded by pilots serving in Northern Ireland, who appreciated its toughness. 'By the most modern standards of technology our Wessex HC2 aircraft are unsophisticated and indeed may be termed geriatric,' wrote the SHDNI's acting OC, Squadron Leader Roberts, in 1979, 'but have long established a reputation for ruggedness and reliability which suit them well to the SH role.'[5]

The second of the RAF's medium transport types deployed to Northern Ireland was the Puma. Developed by Aérospatiale in the 1960s, this twin-engined aircraft entered service with the RAF in 1971 as the Westland Puma HC1, and was capable of carrying sixteen fully equipped troops or around 2,500kg of cargo. Despite its bulky appearance, the Puma was fast and, according to one pilot, 'fantastically responsive'.

To allow crews to operate effectively at night and in poor visibility, night vision goggles (NVGs) were introduced from 1976, while the powerful Nitesun searchlight was fitted to many of the helicopters.

As the demands placed upon the helicopter force increased after the suspension of mobile patrols in South Armagh in the mid-1970s, a detachment of four Royal Navy Wessex HU5s from 845 NAS arrived to augment the RAF's Wessex in November 1977. But there were still complaints that helicopter provision in the border areas was inadequate, Margaret Thatcher's Security Co-ordinator in Northern Ireland Sir Maurice Oldfield pointing out in his Security Review of April 1980 that one of the things the Army had asked for was 'more generous allocation of helicopters'.

The situation was alleviated somewhat by the relocation of 72 Squadron in its entirety to RAF Aldergrove in 1981, bringing the number of Wessex in the province to twenty-one, which now became the Support Helicopter Force Northern Ireland (SHFNI). Air mobility was also given a boost with the introduction of the excellent new Westland Lynx AH1. The extremely fast and highly agile Lynx could carry up to nine troops or 1,360kg of cargo – more than double that of the Scout, which it began to replace as the Army Air Corps' standard utility helicopter in the province from 1979, 654 Squadron becoming the first to operate the Lynx in Northern Ireland in October. That year also saw the various Army Air Corps squadrons and detachments scattered throughout the province come under the new title of Northern Ireland Regiment AAC, a title which remained in use until October 1993, when it was renamed 5 Regiment AAC.

Troops tended to express a preference for Army and especially Royal Navy crews over those of the Royal Air Force, believing the former to be less bound by the rules than their 'light blue' counterparts. The SAS soldier turned author Andy McNab, who in the late 1970s served with the 2nd Bn Royal Green Jackets in South Armagh, rated the Navy crews most highly, considering them 'more daring, and always on time' to extract a patrol.[6]

All crews shared a fear of coming down in Bandit Country, either through mechanical failure or hostile action, and falling into the hands of the IRA. Royal Navy pilot Michael Booth, who flew the Scout on attachment with the AAC in Northern Ireland in the 1970s, said:

> I was always quite worried about crashing in South Armagh and being captured by the IRA ... . Subsequently, being back there many years later, with twin-engined helicopters and guys in the back with machine guns, you felt far more comfortable. In those early days, in a pretty unreliable helicopter, you were certainly less confident.[7]

On 24 August 1979 a Gazelle from 662 Squadron carrying two soldiers of the 1st Bn Queen's Own Highlanders crashed at an isolated spot known as Jerrettspass, near Bessbrook, after hitting power lines, a major hazard for helicopter crews serving in the province and the cause of several crashes. Both of the QOH soldiers were killed and the pilot injured after being flung out of the helicopter upon impact. A group of engineers working nearby rushed to the pilot's aid. But the injured airman, fearing they were IRA, held them at bay with his Browning pistol. 'Immediately he saw us he pulled out a pistol and kept us covered,' one of the men recalled. 'He demanded to know who we were and made us produce our identification papers. Soon afterwards another helicopter landed and took him to hospital.'[8]

In an area measuring only a few hundred square kilometres, there was a finite number of landing sites for helicopters to drop off and pick up patrols, as one RAF officer pointed out: 'South Armagh is a relatively small area for the number of helicopter movements which take place there in any 24 hour period.'[9] But maintaining predictable flight patterns and re-using the same landing sites too often was to invite disaster. In June 1976 a patrol from the 3rd Bn Parachute Regiment was awaiting an extraction from a field at Drumlougher near Cullyhanna, unaware that it had often been used for pick-ups. PIRA had taken note and earlier planted a bomb in a hedgerow. As the paras took up defensive positions before the helicopter's arrival the bomb was triggered, fatally injuring one of the soldiers.

There were also deliberate 'come-ons' – attacks or incidents staged by the IRA with the intention of luring the security forces and their helicopters into ambushes or booby-traps. One such incident took place on 8 February 1974, when a Scout carrying Welsh Guardsmen, responding to a report of bombs having been left in a supermarket at Cullaville, landed in a nearby field in which PIRA had planted eight landmines. In what the Army called 'a mass murder attempt', as the soldiers disembarked from the helicopter the mines were detonated by command wire, fortunately without causing any serious casualties or damaging the helicopter.

Casevac flights

One of the most important roles undertaken by helicopters in South Armagh was casualty evacuation. The lives of hundreds of soldiers and policemen were saved during the 'Troubles' thanks to timely evacuation by helicopter, and numerous awards for gallantry were made to airmen for carrying out especially hazardous casevac missions.

Not all such flights were in response to a terrorist attack. On 16 December 1989 an Army unit was ascending Croslieve Hill near Forkhill to relieve soldiers manning the Golf Four Zero watchtower at the summit of the 308-metre-high hill. The weather was bad, with heavy sleet and gale-force winds. During the ascent one of the soldiers was knocked unconscious after slipping on the wet rock, suffering a suspected skull fracture. Stuck halfway up the hill, in appalling weather conditions, with a seriously injured casualty who couldn't be moved, the unit's commander realized the only hope of saving the soldier was a risky helicopter pick-up.

Major Sam Drennan, a former Scots Guardsman who transferred to the Army Air Corps in 1972, was returning from a patrol in his Lynx when the emergency call came through and volunteered to attempt a pick-up, after another helicopter crew was forced to abandon a rescue due to the conditions. It was now dark, snowing heavily and, even with the night vision goggles he was equipped with, visibility was poor. Nevertheless,

Major Drennan, 'with the greatest skill, determination and daring, edged his aircraft to the pick-up point, talking himself in by radioing to the troops on the ground', explained his award recommendation.

The pilot gently settled the leading edge of the helicopter's skids onto the slopes of the hill, allowing the casualty – who had to be restrained when, in his now semi-conscious and delirious state, he began to thrash around violently – to be embarked. The Lynx then flew back safely to Bessbrook Mill and the injured soldier went on to make a full recovery.

For his 'courage, nerve and outstanding professional skill', which was 'in the very highest aviation and military traditions', Major Drennan was awarded the Air Force Cross in November 1990,[10] complementing the DFC he had earned for a series of daring casevac missions carried out under enemy fire during the Falklands conflict.

Perhaps the most dramatic casevac mission took place a decade earlier, on 27 August 1979. This would prove to be the deadliest day for the British Army in Northern Ireland. Late that afternoon a three-vehicle military convoy carrying men of the 2nd Bn Parachute Regiment was travelling from their base in Ballykinlar, County Down, to Newry. Though considered vulnerable by the Army, the route was still occasionally used by military vehicles.[11] At 1640 hours, as the convoy passed a trailer parked in a lay-by close to Narrow Water Castle, near the town of Warrenpoint, the rearmost lorry was torn apart by a massive explosion. Hidden beneath straw bales on the trailer was a 200kg bomb, detonated using radio control by two PIRA men in the Republic, who were observing the convoy's progress from across Carlingford Lough.

After receiving the contact report, the crew of a Wessex on a routine flight landed at Bessbrook just long enough to embark a medical team led by Captain Barber of the Royal Army Medical Corps and a four-man ARF before rushing to the scene of the attack, accompanied by a Gazelle carrying Lieutenant Colonel David Blair, commanding the 1st Bn Queen's Own Highlanders, the area's resident unit. There they found a scene of utter carnage; six paratroopers were dead and several others seriously wounded. While Captain Barber supervised the loading of the casualties into the Wessex, the Gazelle dropped off Lieutenant Colonel

Blair, who set up an Incident Control Point by the stone gatehouse opposite Narrow Water Castle, and its pilot headed back to Bessbrook.

At 1712 hours, shortly after taking off, the Gazelle's pilot Lieutenant Wilson saw a huge dust cloud rise up into the air from where he had set the CO down a couple of minutes earlier. Behind the gatehouse PIRA had planted a second, even larger bomb, correctly predicting that the surviving soldiers would take cover there. The Wessex was just lifting off with its casualties when this second, 350kg, device exploded, the powerful blast causing it to rock violently in the air. 'Just as we were taking off there was a massive explosion,' Captain Barber recalled at the inquest held the following year. 'The Wessex was blown about by this explosion and turned through 90 degrees.'[12]

The force of the blast blew out one of the helicopter's Perspex windows and it was showered with granite debris from the destroyed gatehouse, one piece – said to be the size of a football – passing through the rotor blades and striking the nose of the helicopter. To those surviving paras watching on the ground, it seemed certain that the aircraft would crash. 'I remember thinking, "Christ, it's not going to make it,"' said one of the paras.[13]

But the pilot successfully maintained control and the wounded Wessex clattered back safely to Bessbrook Mill with its casualties. In the Operations Record Book, 72 Squadron's acting OC Squadron Leader Roberts noted that despite the force of the blast 'the damage sustained to the aircraft was remarkably light', something he attributed to the renowned toughness of the Wessex: 'The limited damage sustained by the aircraft speaks volumes for its rugged construction'.

In all, eighteen soldiers were killed in the double bombing at Warrenpoint, including Lieutenant Colonel Blair, and a further six injured, making it the bloodiest IRA attack on the British Army during the 'Troubles'. But had the second blast brought down the Wessex, it could have been even worse, as Squadron Leader Roberts pointed out: 'We were extremely lucky to have escaped with no injuries to the crew'.[14]

Eye in the sky

From the earliest days of the 'Troubles' aerial observation became a key element of the security forces' counter-terrorism strategy in South

Armagh. To begin with this mainly entailed helicopters flying border patrols, with an observer equipped with nothing more sophisticated than a pair of binoculars, scanning the terrain below. The Westland Sioux proved especially well suited to this kind of work, its Plexiglas bubble canopy affording an excellent all-round view.

Aerial intelligence in Operation BANNER took a leap forward with the establishment of the Reconnaissance Intelligence Centre at RAF Aldergrove in 1973, whose purpose was to process and analyse imagery gathered by aircraft on photo-reconnaissance sorties. Canberra PR9 jets of No.39 Squadron (which became No.1 PRU – Photographic Reconnaissance Unit – in 1982), were used for high-level reconnaissance, operating from their home base at Wyton in Cambridgeshire. For low-to-medium level reconnaissance the RIC had at its disposal Army Scout and RAF Wessex and Puma helicopters, equipped with Vinten F95 cameras. Its principal PR platform, however, was the de Havilland Canada Beaver AL1, a dedicated flight of three such machines drawn from 655 and 669 Squadrons being detached to RAF Aldergrove from October 1973. This was expanded to five aircraft, becoming the Beaver Flight, in March 1976.

This rugged fixed-wing aircraft, powered by a single Pratt & Whitney radial engine, saw service with the Army Air Corps from 1961 to 1989, performing light liaison, communications and, when fitted with an F95 camera, photo-reconnaissance functions in numerous trouble spots around the globe where British forces were deployed, including Borneo (during the Indonesian Confrontation of the mid 1960s) and Aden.

From modest beginnings, with just eight personnel, the RIC quickly grew to satisfy the immense demand for its services, and soon became an indispensable element of the counter-terrorism infrastructure in Northern Ireland. An official crest was conferred upon the unit in 1986, which depicts an owl and carries the apt motto 'Oculis Venamur' ('We hunt with our eyes').

The work of the RIC was particularly important in rural areas like South Armagh, where the imagery collected was used by PIs

(Photographic Interpreters) to identify areas of disturbed earth which might indicate where an IED or its command-wire had been buried.

While the highly sensitive nature of its work means that, even today, much of its equipment and methods remain secret, there's no doubt that the Reconnaissance Intelligence Centre played a major part in foiling many terrorist attacks in Northern Ireland. In 1977 the RIC's work was recognized with the award of the prestigious Wilkinson Battle of Britain Memorial Sword for its 'most valuable contribution towards the development of operational tactics'.

Well aware of the important intelligence-gathering function of the Beaver, the South Armagh brigade occasionally targeted the aircraft when they were carrying out low-level sorties. One such attack occurred on 31 January 1976. Captain Sean Long was on a PR sortie along the South Armagh border in a Beaver when it came under rifle fire, the incident report recording: 'At 1247 hours 7 x HV [High Velocity] shots fired at Beaver aircraft (1 hit)'.[15] A single round pierced the starboard wing but Captain Long made a successful landing back at RAF Aldergrove.

A more dangerous encounter between PIRA gunmen and the crew of a Beaver took place in 1979. At around 1300 hours on 13 November, minutes after a Welsh Guardsman had been killed by an IED at Ford's Cross near Silverbridge, the pilot of a Beaver on patrol just south of Crossmaglen spotted an IVCP manned by a group of nine masked, armed men, who had blocked the road with a car and a van. At the time PIRA were mounting roadblocks with increasing frequency throughout South Armagh to demonstrate their control of the area; on 22 November Secretary of State for Northern Ireland Humphrey Atkins admitted that so far that year four such IVCPs were recorded as having been set up by PIRA in the Crossmaglen area alone. As the pilot brought the Beaver down to 200 feet to photograph the gunmen they opened fire with Armalites and an M60 machine gun, hitting the aircraft six times. One bullet came up through the floor and cut the observer's helmet microphone lead, while another struck the propeller. But the pilot kept control of the Beaver and made a safe landing. [16]

The Invisible Wall

Throughout the 'Troubles' crews had at all times to be conscious of the border with the Republic; the 'Invisible Wall', as some called it. While the IRA were able to move back and forth across the frontier with relative impunity, for British airmen crossing into Irish airspace was strictly prohibited. 'You do not fly across the border,' said one Army Air Corps pilot. 'Border incursion is frowned upon'.

Nevertheless, incursions both in the air and on the ground by foot patrols became relatively common, provoking the ire of the Irish government. In 1976 the Minister for Foreign Affairs, Garret FitzGerald, revealed that British military aircraft had violated Irish airspace on 157 separate occasions over the previous three years.[17] In the Dáil (Irish Parliament) in October 1973 Thomas Meaney of the Fianna Fail party raged: 'The position now is that there is a foreign army flying over our territory ... [the British] are flying regularly over our territory in the border areas. Our citizens and our army object to this.'[18]

In their defence British pilots argued that with only basic navigation equipment to rely on and a poorly defined border, which cuts through villages, farms and streets, inadvertent incursions were unavoidable. 'The border is totally indistinguishable ... it's very easy to cross it by mistake,' explained a British officer. One patrol accidentally dropped off by a Wessex too far south only realized the pilot had deposited them within the Republic's territory after noticing that the telephone boxes were painted green.[19]

But their predicament earned little sympathy from their Irish counterparts. Dublin's attitude hardened further after eight SAS soldiers were arrested by Gardai in May 1976 in what became known as the Flagstaff Hill incident, having strayed across the border while on a covert surveillance operation, and an Army Air Corps helicopter, whose pilot had become lost on a mail run between bases in South Armagh and was running critically low on fuel, made an emergency landing at the Monaghan Army base on 14 June 1977. The helicopter was immediately surrounded by armed soldiers and the two British crewmen sheepishly emerged with their arms raised. 'They were very embarrassed,' recalled one of the Irish soldiers present that day.[20] After refuelling, the crew were allowed to return to Northern Ireland.

The NIO lobbied the Irish government to relax its stance on British military aircraft overflying Irish territory in cases where crews were engaged in 'hot pursuit' of terrorist suspects fleeing across the border following an attack. Writing to Garret FitzGerald in December 1974, Secretary of State for Northern Ireland Merlyn Rees urged greater cross-border security co-operation. 'Without positive action by the security forces of both sides working closely together the situation in Crossmaglen and the border areas will continue to be a constant source of anxiety and challenge to both Governments,' he wrote.[21] But the only concession Dublin was willing to make was to permit limited overflights to check on suspected IEDs or their firing points on the Republic side of the border.

Even this, however, was considered a step too far by the Irish military. In May 1973 Sergeant Major Vines of the 2nd Bn Parachute Regiment was killed by a landmine at Moybane on the County Armagh/Louth border. A second large landmine straddling the border was discovered during the follow-up operation. The British Embassy lodged a request with the Irish Department of Foreign Affairs for an Army helicopter to hover over the area so that an ATO could inspect what was described as a 'particularly complex device' from the air. Permission was granted, only for the Irish Army to object on the grounds that this would constitute a breach of sovereignty, leading to several more hours of bureaucratic wrangling before the Irish Army's objection was finally overruled and the overflight given the go-ahead.[22]

Restrictions on entering Irish airspace were a source of immense frustration to British aircrews, who often had to call off the pursuit of suspects and watch impotently as their quarry escaped across the border. There was also a widespread suspicion that some Irish policemen and soldiers stationed along the border were turning a blind eye to terrorist activity on their side of their border. One Sioux pilot, recalling a firefight he observed near the border between the IRA and British troops in late

1971, after which the gunmen fled south in a car, claimed that, 'The Irish Army and Garda assembled but took no action. I watched as the terrorists' car drove along a minor road in the Republic running parallel to the border, and approached the Irish soldiers and police from behind. They then got out and casually waved to me. All I could do was fly up and down giving a running commentary to our people on the ground, but they were equally powerless.'[23]

The perceived lack of co-operation from their Irish counterparts led the British Army to try to stem the cross-border movement of terrorists and arms by blowing craters in the 200 or so unapproved crossings along the border, many of which were in South Armagh. Condemning the move, Taoiseach Jack Lynch warned the policy would merely 'aggravate a deteriorating situation'. British diplomats were also sceptical. Sir John Peck, UK Ambassador to Dublin, stated in a letter to the FCO that he didn't believe road-cratering 'would be more than a harassment' to the IRA.[24] But in October 1971 the British Army pressed ahead with the plan, known as the Ashburton Programme. As the scheme's critics feared, it damaged Anglo-Irish relations without significantly curbing IRA activity on the border and the programme was later abandoned.

Until there was a significant improvement in co-operation between the security forces of the two countries, for the British the problem of South Armagh's lawless frontier would remain.

Chapter Four

Pot-shots

As the violence intensified and helicopters became a constant presence in Northern Ireland's skies, it wasn't long before they began to attract hostile attention from gunmen on the ground. Pilots first reported coming under fire while flying observation patrols over Belfast and Londonderry in their Sioux helicopters in the summer of 1970. During what became known as the battle of the Lower Falls, a night of intense rioting on 3 July in west Belfast's nationalist Falls Road, shots were fired at a Sioux carrying Brigadier Peter Hudson, commander of 39 Infantry Brigade, which was circling overhead. Fearing – incorrectly, as it turned out – that his aircraft had been hit, the pilot made an emergency landing.

The weapons at the disposal of the IRA at this time typically consisted of Second World War-vintage rifles like the M1 Garand and Lee-Enfield .303, along with sub-machine guns like the famous Thompson. The shooting was generally inaccurate and by maintaining an altitude of 1,500 feet crews were, in the words of one AAC pilot, 'virtually safe from any musketry the IRA can muster'. In a 1972 edition of the *Army Air Corps Journal*, 651 Squadron OC Major Palmer wrote: 'Some of their gunmen seem overconfident in the capabilities of a Thompson sub-machine gun fired at an aircraft some 1,500 feet overhead. One warrior was even observed engaging a Sioux at 1,200 feet with a pistol!'[1]

Often pilots weren't even aware of having come under attack. 'I had small arms fired at me over Belfast and certainly in Londonderry during [Operation] MOTORMAN. And the only time you'd ever know is when someone on the ground would tell you. In a helicopter you can't hear anyone firing at you,' explained Royal Navy pilot Michael Booth. 'Of course,' he added, 'the IRA are just pot-shotting at you. The chance of them being successful are pretty slim.'[2]

For the IRA, these pot-shot attacks in the cities were carried out more as an act of defiance to raise morale than in any expectation of bringing a helicopter down. Brendan Hughes, a senior figure in the Belfast PIRA, recalled how he gave a distraught female volunteer who had just witnessed one of her comrades being killed in a gun battle with British troops a Garand rifle and ordered her to open fire at a helicopter hovering some distance above. 'Not that it was going to do any good; she wasn't going to bring the helicopter down,' he admitted, 'but it helped to control her emotions.'[3]

Occasionally, however, the bullets did find their mark. In Londonderry on 13 January 1972, a Sioux of the Royal Marines' Kangaw Flight, 3 CBAS carrying out a reconnaissance of the city was called in by a patrol of the 1st Bn Coldstream Guards to help pinpoint the location of a gunman they had been chasing in the city's Creggan district. In his subsequent Hostile Action Report, the Royal Marine pilot stated, 'I located the gunman and was asked to direct our own forces against him.' As he did so more gunmen arrived on the scene (from both the Official and Provisional IRA) and a major firefight erupted between the Guardsmen and the terrorists, during which shots were fired at the Sioux. 'I returned to base after max endurance on task and although I had been informed that my A/C had come under fire during the sortie, I was not aware of having been hit until after I had landed at base,' the pilot reported. An inspection of the Sioux revealed that a single bullet had holed the synchronized elevator, which Kangaw Flight's OC considered 'a very lucky shot'.[4]

As the violence in Londonderry spiralled out of control during the first half of 1972, the British Army responded by launching Operation CARCAN in the early hours of 31 July. This was part of the wider Operation MOTORMAN, involving thousands of troops backed up by Centurion AVREs and helicopters serving as airborne command posts, to re-establish control in the 'no-go' areas of west Belfast and so-called 'Free Derry', where PIRA were operating openly. In advance of the operation, a Canberra PR9 also flew reconnaissance sorties from England, helping to detect terrorist weapons caches.

Troops encountered virtually no resistance from the IRA when they moved in, though Scout pilot Michael Booth recalled coming under fire at one point while flying over Londonderry: 'I flew a lot during that night of operations... I was flying a senior officer, a battalion commander, around Londonderry for most of the night. We were flying above the Creggan, being shot at .... At the end of that I was mentioned in despatches.'[5]

The re-imposition of the Army's authority in Londonderry and west Belfast following Operations CARCAN and MOTORMAN forced the IRA underground, and, together with a belated realization of the calamitous effect on their support should they succeed in shooting a helicopter down over a heavily-populated nationalist neighbourhood, led to IRA attacks on helicopters flying over Northern Ireland's two main cities virtually ceasing after the summer of 1972.

But in the thinly populated rural border areas, where the risk of collateral damage was far smaller, the IRA's war against British helicopters was only just beginning.

'Pirate Sky Ships'

An insight into IRA strategy at this time was gained by the security forces when they captured a copy of a manual instructing volunteers on guerrilla warfare tactics. Written around 1971, of particular interest was a section devoted to the British Army's use of helicopters:

> The 'border' of Ireland is being more and more brought under the surveillance of the occupation army using helicopters. These vehicles are vulnerable to the shots of a skilled marksman. In the Vietnamese liberation over 800 helicopters have been disposed of by guerrillas since 1967. If we can achieve a rate of destruction equal to only one quarter of this, the presence of these pirate sky ships over our country will be removed, in a few months.

In fact, the author greatly underestimated the helicopter losses suffered by the US during the Vietnam War; by the early 1970s the Americans had lost around 2,000 rotary-wing aircraft in combat. The manual went on to advise volunteers on the most effective means of bringing down helicopters with small arms:

> The point of attack for your bullets on a helicopter is the rotor arm. One strike on this will disable the propellers. Firing through the Perspex visor can kill the pilot, but shots at the belly of the craft are likely to be deflected by sheet steel fitted for that purpose. So make your mark the rotor arm. Shots aimed at this will, if they miss, go unheard by the pilot. The one he does hear will be the one that will force his craft back to earth. When his craft does crash a small PE [plastic explosive] charge set in the engine space will put it out of action for good.[6]

In South Armagh and the other border areas the IRA were not slow in putting the theory to the test. The main targets were Sioux carrying out visual reconnaissance and providing top cover for patrols along the border with the Irish Republic. On 9 October 1970 a Sioux searching for terrorists who had blown up a customs post in County Fermanagh was attacked by gunmen firing from the village of Cloghoge just across the border in County Cavan, one of the rounds hitting the aircraft's radio. A year later, in one of the first recorded helicopter attacks in County Armagh, fifteen to twenty shots were fired at a helicopter called in to support an RUC patrol under attack in Forkhill on 19 September 1971. The helicopter wasn't hit and the IRA attackers fled across the border. This set the pattern for future attacks, with the IRA escaping into the relative sanctuary of the Irish Republic after attacking helicopters patrolling the border.

On 13 October 1971, in one of the largest gun battles of the conflict up to that point, sappers preparing to blow a crater in an unapproved road were ambushed by a force of around forty IRA gunmen at Dungooley, on the border between County Armagh and Louth. During the hour-long gun battle that followed a helicopter providing support for the sappers came under fire and was forced to withdraw. On the same day, a Sioux flown by Captain Tim Holmes of the Queen's Dragoon Guards

Air Squadron, covering another road-cratering operation in County Tyrone, came under small-arms fire from three gunmen at Castlederg. Captain Holmes was forced to make a precautionary landing six miles away, where an inspection of the aircraft revealed that it had been hit by two bullets, one of which was lodged in the engine.

More shootings followed in 1972, with South Armagh now emerging as a hotspot for helicopter attacks. On 10 August a Sioux was fired at whilst responding to an attack on a VCP in Crossmaglen, forcing the pilot to pull out, and three weeks later another came under fire during a pursuit of a suspect car with no number plates near Forkhill, which escaped across the border. No hits were registered on either occasion.

But the marksmanship of the South Armagh brigade's gunmen was improving all the time, and on the morning of 14 December 1972 a helicopter was hit by small-arms fire for the first time in South Armagh. The helicopter, a Sioux of 654 Squadron, came in low to photograph a suspicious lorry parked near Crossmaglen when several PIRA men armed with Garand rifles opened fire, one of the rounds ricocheting off the seat armour and slightly injuring the observer. 'Six shots hit the helicopter and a passenger suffered a grazed thigh,' confirmed the Hostile Action Report. The pilot made an emergency landing at the Crossmaglen base, and an examination of the aircraft found damage to the main rotor blades, bubble canopy and stabilizer bar. Four men were arrested an hour after the attack by Gardaí just across the border at Courtbane and several Garands recovered. Though not made public at the time, according to the Army's report into the incident, 'The pilot also reported the flash and bang of a rocket launcher being fired and a missile is thought to have exploded in front of the aircraft.'[7] The Provisionals had acquired several Russian-made RPG-7 rocket launchers earlier that year, probably from sources in Algeria, and they were first used in an attack on an RUC station in Fermanagh in November, in which a policeman was killed.

It wasn't just in the air that crews were at risk. Republican terrorists increasingly targeted military personnel when off-duty. After a night out at the Knock-Na-Moe Castle Hotel bar in Omagh on 17 May 1973, two Scout pilots serving with 652 Squadron, Staff Sergeant Arthur Place of the Prince of Wales's Own Regiment of Yorkshire and Royal Marine Sergeant Derek Reed, were killed along with two other soldiers attached to the Army Air Corps by a booby-trap bomb rigged to their car. An RUC officer who attended the scene described it as 'one of absolute carnage. I have never seen anything quite like it in my service'.[8]

The British Army responded to the growing threat from small-arms fire by issuing new guidelines for crews stationed in Northern Ireland in October 1971. Pilots were prohibited from flying below 1,500 feet over any 'sensitive area' and instructed to wear flak-jackets when flying border patrols. Additional armour plating was also added beneath the seats, as well as to the backrests, although the additional weight inevitably meant a penalty had to be paid in reduced performance and carrying capacity. For self-defence should they be forced down in hostile areas, pilots were also ordered to carry a Browning 9mm pistol and one full magazine on all sorties.[9]

But thoughts were already turning to equipping helicopter crews with more substantial firepower.

Gunships in Ulster?

In November 1971 the Army conducted a demonstration for the benefit of the press at its firing range at Magilligan Point, on the north coast of County Londonderry, of Sioux and Scout helicopters armed with GPMGs. The object of the exercise, according to the monthly flight report of the Royal Marines' 3 CBAS, was: 'To obtain press coverage and thus remind the IRA that helicopters (which they shoot at with increasing regularity) do have a capability to hit back'.[10]

One of these demonstration flights was carried out by Major Gradidge of the 17th/21st Lancers Air Squadron, in a Sioux AH1. 'As a general rule we would fire only at someone who was shooting at us first, and only if we had a clearly defined target,' he assured the assembled journalists.

But as the reporters witnessed tracer rounds from the helicopters ricocheting wildly off the ground at Magilligan Point, the demonstration served only to confirm in the minds of most of those present that the armed helicopter was an indiscriminate weapon, unsuitable for use in Northern Ireland.

The media's negative reaction discouraged the Army from pursuing the idea. But in 1973 the question of arming helicopters was resurrected when a new GOC arrived at HQNI in Lisburn, County Antrim. General Sir Frank King was a para who had fought at Arnhem in the Second World War and, as a qualified helicopter pilot who would later serve as Colonel Commandant of the Army Air Corps, was reportedly keen to expand the role of aviation in the fight against terrorism in Northern Ireland.

A few weeks after taking up his appointment, HQNI submitted a paper to Defence Secretariat 10 (DS10), an MoD department which liaised between the Army and British government on military matters regarding Northern Ireland, setting out the case for the arming of helicopters operating in the largely lawless border regions 'to provide the deterrence, observation and rapid follow-up capability so urgently required to defeat the hit-and-run gunman in rural areas'.[11]

Soldiers on board helicopters were already permitted to fire their SLRs at targets on the ground – so long as that target could be clearly identified as an armed terrorist who presented an immediate threat – and on occasion had done so. On 3 November 1972 troops on board a Scout returned fire after coming under attack from seven PIRA gunmen at Moybane near Crossmaglen. Neither the helicopter nor any of the attackers were hit.

Helicopters were also used in more unorthodox offensive actions. During a cordon and search operation conducted by the security forces in June 1973 to round up a large number of PIRA suspects in south County Londonderry, two terrorist suspects attempted to flee by boat across Lough Neagh. The pilot of a Sioux tried to use the rotor downwash to force the vessel back towards the soldiers waiting on the shore, an attempt which the suspects defeated by dropping anchor. But then a twin-engined Puma of the RAF's 33 Squadron joined in, its much more powerful downwash almost causing the boat to capsize and forcing the suspects to surrender.

Helicopters of the SHDNI were also called in to help put down a major riot by republican prisoners at the Long Kesh Detention Centre in

County Down. At around 1800 hours on 15 October 1974, hundreds of IRA inmates overpowered their guards and went on the rampage, setting fire to their compounds. The riot had been well planned, the prisoners having secretly amassed an arsenal of improvised weapons, such as poles with large nails fixed to the end; 'in fact,' recalled one soldier of the Duke of Edinburgh's Royal Regiment, which was rushed to the scene to deal with the trouble, 'they were better armed than we were with just our wooden batons'.[12]

Chaotic hand-to-hand fighting raged between the troops and the prisoners throughout the night and into the next day, and casualties mounted on both sides. With the outnumbered soldiers on the point of being overwhelmed, Wessex helicopters arrived from Aldergrove and began dropping canisters of CS gas onto the rioters. The timely intervention of the helicopters, together with the arrival of reinforcements, finally brought the riot to an end.

But deploying armed aircraft to combat insurgents within the United Kingdom was politically a highly sensitive issue, particularly at a time when images of US gunships unleashing massive firepower into the Vietnamese jungle were playing regularly on TV news reports. Recognizing this, the paper's author was at pains to draw a distinction between the Americans' use of heavily-armed gunships in south-east Asia and what was being envisaged for Northern Ireland. 'The term "gunship" which is frequently heard in this context is misleading,' the HQNI paper stated, 'because it gives the impression of saturation fire from the equivalent of the American Cobra.'

Instead, what the Army proposed was equipping their Sioux helicopters with a single swivel-mounted GPMG, with the main target being 'the gunman engaging Security Forces in open rural areas'.

The belt-fed 7.62mm General Purpose Machine Gun, nicknamed the 'Gimpy' by British troops, was the standard infantry support weapon of the British Army, with a rate of fire of around 800 rounds per minute. While accepting that pinpoint accuracy with such a weapon fired from a hovering helicopter was not possible, the author insisted that 'with a trained gunner, an acceptable degree of accuracy can be achieved' and that 'under carefully but easily controlled circumstances the use of the system would be entirely within the limitations of the Yellow Card'.

It was also argued that arming helicopters would prove a powerful deterrent to terrorists. 'The presence of even an unarmed helicopter in support of a patrol always has a deterrent effect,' the paper claimed. '... The knowledge that GPMGs are carried in helicopters, and could be used, would be an even greater deterrent and would increase the safety of both the ground troops and aircraft.'

The author had even given some thought as to how to counter the inevitable republican propaganda which would seek to draw parallels between British armed helicopters in Northern Ireland and US gunships in Vietnam, suggesting that a cine camera could be mounted on each armed Sioux 'to show what little fire had been applied'.[13]

But while acknowledging that armed helicopters would offer the security forces a tactical advantage in areas like South Armagh, there was considerable nervousness about the proposal on the part of the NIO, shared by the Foreign Office's Republic of Ireland Department. An official from the latter observed in a letter dated 17 May 1973 that 'such a machine has emotional political connotations' and 'we stand to lose a lot when the IRA propaganda machine gets to work'.[14] More alarming still was the prospect of a British helicopter inadvertently straying across the border whilst engaging gunmen on the ground and hitting an innocent bystander, with the head of DS10, Anthony Stephens, pointing out that 'the political implications of an Eire citizen being shot from a helicopter which turned out to be over Eire territory hardly bear thinking about'.[15]

A suggested compromise of substituting the fully automatic GPMG with a rifle firing single shots from a swivel mount – which, DS10 felt, would 'still provide a valuable deterrent without risking the accusation of escalating the situation' – was looked upon more favourably by the NIO. But this option met with little enthusiasm from the senior advisor to the GOC Northern Ireland, who wrote that, in his view, the idea of helicopters 'armed with swivel mounted rifles intended to operate within existing Yellow Card rules' would be 'both impractical and ineffective,'[16] as the Sioux wasn't felt to be a sufficiently stable platform from which to make accurate sniping attacks.

In the face of opposition from the NIO and Foreign Office, HQNI dropped its calls for armed helicopters. 'In view of [NIO and FO's concerns] we do not wish to persevere with the proposal to arm helicopters in border areas at this stage,' a senior officer wrote to DS10 on 29 May 1973.[17]

The IRA, however, had no such qualms about carrying out attacks from the air, as the security forces would soon discover.

The Irish Republican Air Force

Ian Swales thought his bombing days were long behind him. In 1974 the 59-year-old Englishman was working as the Chief Flying Instructor at the little Dundalk Aero Club in County Louth, after a distinguished career in the RAF that saw him rise from an aircraft apprentice when he joined the service in 1931 to group captain when he retired in 1963.

Qualifying as a pilot shortly before the outbreak of the Second World War, he carried out many raids on targets in Nazi-occupied Europe, flying first Wellingtons with 15 Squadron and later Lancasters with 622 Squadron. By the end of the war he was a wing commander and recipient of the DSO, DFC and DFM, the citation for his DFC stating: 'This officer has always shown courage and determination in the face of the enemy'. Thirty years later, in September 1974, the veteran airman would be forced against his will to carry out one last bombing raid, this time on the orders of the IRA.

The Provisionals' interest in airborne operations began a year earlier. During the afternoon exercise period on 31 October 1973 warders and inmates alike at Dublin's top security Mountjoy prison looked on in astonishment as an Alouette helicopter appeared overhead and landed in the prison yard. By the time the warders had recovered from their initial surprise, three prisoners – all senior members of the Provisional IRA, including its chief of staff Seamus Twomey – had been whisked away in the helicopter. The Alouette had been hijacked earlier that afternoon by a PIRA gang, who forced the pilot to fly them to Mountjoy prison so they could spring their imprisoned comrades from the jail. The daring escape made headlines around the world and immediately entered republican folklore, even inspiring a popular song by Irish republican band The Wolfe Tones.

Encouraged by the success of the helicopter escape, three weeks later Seamus Twomey gave an interview while on the run to the West German *Der Spiegel* magazine, in which he boasted that PIRA would shortly 'fight from the air'. Asked by the interviewer if the Provos were planning to create 'a Republican Air Force', Twomey replied, 'That might be an exaggeration. But,' he promised, 'we will carry out commando operations from the air.'[18]

The security forces didn't have to wait long to find out just what Twomey meant. On 24 January 1974 a Bo 105 helicopter was hijacked by an IRA gang in County Donegal, who jammed a pistol in the side of the pilot, John Hobday, and ordered him to fly them across the border into neighbouring County Tyrone. Among the four hijackers was Rose Dugdale, a 32-year-old English heiress and former debutante, who had rejected her privileged upbringing and joined PIRA. Hovering over the RUC station in the town of Strabane, Dugdale and her accomplices heaved two milk churns packed with explosives out of the helicopter. One of the bombs landed within a few metres of the station but neither exploded. Despite the failure, in an interview almost forty years later Dugdale insisted that the raid 'probably had an effect on the Brits; that they needed to defend their encampments from the air as well'.[19]

After the raid the helicopter landed at Cloughfin in County Donegal and the gang escaped, leaving the pilot shaken but unhurt. Rose Dugdale's exploit briefly turned her into Britain and Ireland's most wanted woman, until she was captured four months later in County Cork.

It was now clear to the British that Twomey's threats had not been mere bluster. The Army released a statement, explaining that they had not opened fire on the helicopter for fear of causing civilian casualties on the ground should it crash, but went on to warn that 'Such restraint is unlikely to be shown again. Any hostile aircraft or helicopter may in future be engaged with fire'.[20]

In the wake of the air raid, flying restrictions were imposed on civil aircraft in Northern Ireland, including a ban on flying below 2,000 feet near military installations. For months afterwards the situation in Ulster's skies remained tense. Pilots of privately-owned light aircraft complained of being buzzed by British military helicopters, even when flying outside the restricted zones, and flying clubs north and south of the border were regularly visited by the RUC and Garda to check that their aircraft were secure. There were even reports that machine guns for air defence had been mounted on the roofs of some military bases in the province and several helicopters were equipped with GPMGs to intercept airborne IRA raiders – though mindful of the earlier opposition to armed helicopters from the NIO and Foreign Office, HQNI made clear that 'use of GPMGs from hels [helicopters] is authorised only against aircraft attacking SF bases'.[21]

Their caution was justified, for, despite the failure of the Dugdale bombing mission, PIRA were planning another air raid on a security forces base, this time in South Armagh.

At around 1900 hours on Saturday 28 September 1974, the relaxed atmosphere in the clubhouse of the Dundalk Aero Club was suddenly shattered when four masked PIRA volunteers burst in, waving guns and demanding to know who among the eight startled club members was the most experienced pilot. Retired Group Captain Ian Swales stepped forward. While two of the gang stayed behind to guard the remaining hostages, the other two gunmen loaded four canisters into the flying club's little Socata Rallye four-seat trainer plane and forced Swales at gunpoint to fly them north, following the Dublin to Belfast railway into South Armagh.

PIRA's ambitious plan was to co-ordinate a simultaneous air and ground attack on a hilltop Army observation post at Drumackavall near Crossmaglen, manned at the time by Royal Marines. But while the ground assault phase went ahead as planned, with an estimated force of twenty guerrillas firing twenty-three mortars at the OP before raking it with automatic gunfire, the airborne element of the attack quickly turned into a fiasco.

The hijackers gave Swales conflicting directions and they soon became hopelessly lost. In frustration the PIRA men pushed one of the bombs out of the aircraft – ignoring Swales's desperate warning that opening the cockpit door in flight could destabilize the plane – where it bounced off the wing. Swales later told the press, 'it was lucky that we were not all blown to pieces at that stage.' The bomb fell onto a country lane in Jonesborough, more than ten miles from the intended target, without exploding.

After telling his captors that he was running low on fuel, Swales was then ordered to land. In what he later described as one of the roughest landings of his career, Swales put the Rallye down in a farmer's field in the County Louth village of Ravensdale, coming to rest in a corner of the field. The hijackers fled, leaving behind the three remaining explosive canisters, which Swales himself gingerly removed from the plane. 'I had no time to feel afraid as I moved the bombs from the plane once we had landed,' he told the press.[22] The single bomb dropped by the hijackers was later blown up by an Army EOD team.

With the embarrassing failure of this second air raid, the Provisionals' brief flirtation with airborne operations came to an end. But the South Armagh brigade's campaign against British military aircraft was just beginning. And their attacks were set to become much more dangerous.

Chapter Five

Priority Target

Having turned the roads of South Armagh into no-go areas for the Army, PIRA's next step was to make the skies over Bandit Country just as dangerous, as Eamon McGuire, a former engineer with the Irish airline Aer Lingus (and alleged by the CIA to have been PIRA's 'chief technical officer'), recognized: '[The British Army's] operations were now very dependent on their air superiority. If we wanted to advance to the next phase of the struggle we had to neutralize their air superiority.'[1] In 1977 the South Armagh brigade publicly declared their intent by issuing a statement warning that British helicopters were now 'a priority target'.

For crews serving in the area, this was hardly news. Since 1974 it had become clear that the South Armagh brigade was intensifying their campaign against military aircraft, with the largely unco-ordinated pot-shot attacks carried out by one or two gunmen giving way to better planned, larger scale shoots involving sizeable groups of volunteers, equipped with modern US Armalite assault rifles, which PIRA began to receive from their Irish-American supporters in the early 1970s.

The first of these more determined attacks took place on the evening of 6 April 1974, when a group of gunmen fired over one hundred rounds at an AAC Sioux flying low on border patrol south of Crossmaglen, several of which hit the helicopter, without causing injury.[2]

PIRA then switched their attention to the Army's troop-carrying Scout helicopters. A small-arms attack was carried out on a Scout on 14 December 1975, south-west of Crossmaglen, slightly injuring one of the crew and forcing the pilot to make a precautionary landing, where he found that his aircraft had been hit by two bullets. This attack came at a time when PIRA were supposedly observing a ceasefire, called earlier in the year to allow negotiations to take place with the British government.

The ceasefire, tenuous at best throughout Northern Ireland, was totally ignored in South Armagh, where attacks continued unabated, as Merlyn Rees admitted in November, after three soldiers of the Royal Regiment of Fusiliers were killed in their covert OP at Drumackavall in an assault carried out by up to twelve PIRA gunmen. 'There has never been a ceasefire in South Armagh, for a variety of reasons – the nature of the IRA [there], the nature of the countryside and the nature of the people,' he stated.[3] Frustrated by what it considered a lack of political progress, the 'ceasefire' was officially called off by PIRA on 23 January 1976, by which time it had long since broken down.

Eight days later, on 31 January 1976 (the same day that Captain Long's de Havilland Beaver was hit – see Chapter Three), another Scout came under fire near the border with County Louth. The incident report recorded that approximately thirty rounds were fired at the helicopter from a firing point close to the Kilnasaggart Bridge, near Jonesborough, of which three hit the aircraft, without causing any injuries.

The first DFC

The most significant of the small-arms attacks on helicopters during this period occurred on 3 September 1974, and resulted in the award of the first Distinguished Flying Cross of Operation BANNER.

That afternoon WO2 William Scarratt of 655 Squadron was flying a four-man brick of Royal Marines into a field in the South Armagh village of Ballsmill, just 200 metres from the border with County Louth. But Scarratt, his instincts honed from the twelve years he had served in the Parachute Regiment before joining the AAC in 1970, sensed that something wasn't quite right. 'There were no animals in the fields and no people moving about: a sure sign of trouble,' he explained in an interview thirty-eight years later. His suspicions were further aroused when he noticed that the windows of two nearby houses were flung wide open, even though they appeared to be unoccupied. 'I smelt a rat,' he said.

Rather than land in the exposed open field, Scarratt elected to drop off the patrol a short distance away, where trees and bushes offered some cover. The Royal Marines leapt from the Scout as soon as its skids touched the ground, covering one another with their SLRs. The pilot's suspicions about the apparently vacant houses proved well-founded. As he began lifting off again 'my helicopter was hit by small-arms' fire, coming from one of the two houses,' he revealed. 'I could hear the effects of the hits on the airframe.'

He gave the Scout full power, its Rolls-Royce Nimbus engine straining as he climbed rapidly and, once out of range of the ground-fire, headed back to his base at Forkhill, two miles away. Aside from radio failure, caused by a bullet cutting through his helmet radio microphone lead, 'the aircraft didn't appear to be affected, according to the instruments which I monitored as I flew.'[4]

At the time an Army spokesman merely confirmed that several shots 'passed through the fuselage of the craft'. But an inspection of the aircraft after landing safely back at the Forkhill base revealed the full extent of the damage. Of the eighty-eight rounds fired by the terrorists, six had struck the Scout, damaging the main rotor blades and puncturing the tanks, causing fuel to leak out. Back at the scene of the attack, meanwhile, the Royal Marine patrol returned fire but the gunmen were able to pull out and escape in a waiting car, which sped away across the border. Scarratt's caution in not landing in the open ground, where the hidden PIRA gunmen would have had a much better field of fire, almost certainly saved the helicopter.

The award of the DFC to Warrant Officer Scarratt was announced on 25 March 1975, the recommendation stating that his 'professionalism and coolness both under fire and afterwards were of the highest order', and commended his decision to fly the damaged Scout back to Forkhill, thereby saving his aircraft. 'The alternative to this action, and probably less dangerous from a personal point of view,' the recommendation pointed out, 'would have been to land and abandon the aircraft immediately. In this event the helicopter would undoubtedly have been destroyed by hostile ground fire, a noticeable (*sic*) success of the terrorists. WO2 Scarratt's gallant action was a blow to the terrorists' avowed aim to destroy a helicopter.'[5]

For the first few years of the 'Troubles', the aircraft of the RAF's SHDNI had managed to avoid the hostile attentions of the South Armagh brigade. However, that all changed on 15 April 1976, when a Wessex became the target of the most serious attack on a British helicopter so far.

At 1945 hours a Wessex was flying over the Gaelic football pitch outside the security forces base in Crossmaglen, where it was due to collect a patrol of soldiers from the 3rd Bn Parachute Regiment, when it was hit by a rocket-propelled grenade fired from a building close to the pitch. The pilot, Flight Lieutenant Mike Johnston, recalled:

> We were lucky – we were effectively in the flare. I believe the rocket itself was well targeted. However, as it entered what was the downwash of the helicopter it was deflected downwards and struck the lower step and the fuel pipeline that ran underneath the helicopter.[6]

Fortunately, the warhead of the rocket failed to detonate when it hit the helicopter. As the Wessex bucked under the impact of the rocket, the crew initially thought the aircraft was suffering a mechanical failure. But then several PIRA gunmen positioned nearby followed up the attack with small-arms fire, riddling the Wessex. 'It was only when the bullets started hitting the tail of the helicopter and making their way down towards the main cabin that we realized that we were under attack,' explained Johnston. The crew rapidly set the damaged helicopter down in the base and took cover, as paras stationed at Crossmaglen engaged the gunmen in what an official report later described as 'a fierce gun battle … in which some 500 rounds had been exchanged', forcing the attackers to withdraw. Despite another patrol setting up a roadblock the gunmen successfully slipped away across the border.

The crew had been exceptionally fortunate. 'We lost the starboard engine and there was a lot of bullet damage … but there were no real injuries,' Johnston revealed.[7] When he saw the bullet-riddled Wessex sitting on the helipad, Captain Tony Clarke, one of the paras based at Crossmaglen, realized just how lucky they had been. Had the Wessex been full of troops, he later said, they would have undoubtedly suffered heavy casualties.[8]

The paras secured the surrounding area. But their problems weren't over yet. With the landing site blocked by the stricken Wessex, helicopter movements in and out of Crossmaglen were paralyzed until it could be moved. When he was alerted to the situation at the base, the officer commanding the RAF's SHDNI immediately left Bessbrook Mill for Crossmaglen with a team of ground crew to carry out an inspection of the helicopter. By the time he arrived at the base it was dark and the atmosphere was tense following the attack. An inspection revealed that one of the fuel lines was ruptured, having been hit by the tail fin of the rocket, while small-arms fire had also damaged the tail rotor cable. Despite the extensive damage, he opted to fly the shot-up Wessex to Bessbrook Mill, some eleven miles away. The events that followed were outlined in the recommendation for the DFC he was subsequently put forward for:

> He asked for and obtained the willing support of the second pilot and crewman to accompany him. He lifted out of Crossmaglen at night on both engines but because of damage to the fuel system, he had to close one engine down at 1500 feet before continuing the flight to Bessbrook where he made a safe landing.

At Bessbrook Mill emergency repairs were carried out and three days later the SHDNI CO flew it on to RAF Aldergrove, where it was transported back to England for an extensive overhaul. The award recommendation continued:

> [The pilot] instantly rose to the difficult situation which presented itself at Crossmaglen: his brave decision, made in the knowledge that his personal safety was at considerable risk, was a magnificent example of leadership and devotion to duty. As a result of this commendable action not only was the risk of further attack on a damaged aircraft averted, but also the Provisional IRA were deprived of the considerable prestige which they would

have accrued from their sympathisers had they been able to claim the destruction of a Security Forces helicopter.[9]

Concluding that the leadership displayed by the SHDNI CO was 'in accord with the finest traditions of the Royal Air Force', he was strongly recommended for the Distinguished Flying Cross. On this occasion, however, the award of the DFC ultimately was not approved by the awards committee.

So far, British helicopter crews serving in South Armagh had been extremely fortunate. But their long run of good fortune was soon to come to an end.

'Lt Col Corden-Lloyd was killed in a flying accident – I repeat, a flying accident' British Army spokesman

17 February 1978 was a notable day for the South Armagh brigade. After almost a decade of conflict, on that day they finally succeeded in bringing down a British helicopter, though the circumstances surrounding the crash of Gazelle XX404 would be disputed by the British Army for many years afterwards.

The events leading to the loss of the Gazelle began when a close observation platoon from the 2nd Bn Royal Green Jackets, dug into positions around the Edenappa Road in Jonesborough, was ambushed by PIRA shortly after 1600 hours, who engaged the soldiers with Armalites and an M60 machine gun from behind the March Wall, a stone wall close to, and running parallel with, the border.

The South Armagh village, described in an Army report as 'a notoriously hostile part of the Province', had been the scene of a helicopter attack four months earlier, when a Wessex was hit by a PIRA sniper on 4 October 1977 as it came in to land in a field. On that occasion the only damage was a shattered windscreen. But on this day, the South Armagh brigade would enjoy much greater success.

When the contact report from the Green Jackets' COP team reached the battalion's CO Lieutenant Colonel Ian Corden-Lloyd at Bessbrook

Mill, he rushed to the scene with his adjutant Captain Schofield in a Gazelle of 657 Squadron flown by Sergeant Brian Ives, which was joined by a Scout carrying the ARF.

The stylish Aérospatiale Gazelle AH1 served with both the Army Air Corps and the Royal Marines' 3 CBAS, replacing the Sioux in the liaison and observation roles in Northern Ireland from 1976. Powered by a single Turbomeca turboshaft engine, giving it an impressive top speed of 193mph, the sporty Gazelle was popular with pilots, despite its lack of robustness. 'Light and fragile, but fast and manoeuvrable', was how one Royal Marine pilot described it.[10]

Flying at an altitude of fifty feet, at a speed of 140mph, the Gazelle arrived over the scene of the firefight a few minutes later. Lieutenant Colonel Corden-Lloyd scanned the area below, trying to locate the positions of the gunmen. 'Having made one pass from north to south the CO saw nothing, and requested that they go back along the border again, heading north,' explained the Board of Inquiry's report into the incident.[11]

Tracer rounds then flashed past the cockpit as the helicopter began attracting fire from a PIRA member manning the M60. Sergeant Ives immediately took evasive action, making a sharp climbing turn. But the manoeuvre went wrong, as the report disclosed: 'During this turn the nose of the aircraft fell steeply and XX404 started to dive towards the ground.'[12] After hitting the ground, the helicopter momentarily rose back into the air before smashing back down again, cartwheeling across a field and finally coming to rest 100 metres away.

The four-man ARF (a medic and three soldiers of the 2nd Bn Light Infantry) was dropped by the Scout close by. Under fire from the PIRA gunmen, they raced over to the crash site, extricated Corden-Lloyd and Captain Schofield from the mangled wreckage and hauled them into the cover of a nearby ditch. As more soldiers from the Light Infantry arrived in a Wessex, Sergeant Ives, who was trapped under the wreckage, was also pulled free and the PIRA attackers melted away into the Dromad Wood behind the March Wall. Schofield and Ives were both badly injured, but as he examined Corden-Lloyd the medic could find no signs of life. All three were evacuated to Belfast's Musgrave Park Hospital, where, the official report stated, 'Lieutenant Colonel Ian Corden-Lloyd was confirmed dead on arrival'.[13] He was buried with full military honours in Magdalene Hill cemetery in Winchester.

The loss of the most senior British officer killed in action in Northern Ireland since the 'Troubles' began had an immediate political impact. In the House of Commons on 21 February, Under-Secretary of State for the Army, Robert Brown, paid tribute to the Colonel, describing him as 'a superb commanding officer, a very great and gallant soldier,' and adding: 'The Army and the nation are much the poorer with his untimely passing'.[14]

The apparent downing of the helicopter, along with the massacre of twelve civilians in a PIRA bomb attack at the La Mon House hotel in County Down that same day, led the Shadow Secretary of State for Northern Ireland, Airey Neave, who would himself be assassinated by republican terrorists the following year, to call for tougher action against the IRA. Warning that the downing of the helicopter 'could have serious implications for the security forces', he also declared that the use of an M60 machine gun – several of which had reached the Provisionals after being stolen in a raid on a National Guard armoury in Massachusetts – 'added a new dimension to the security problem'.[15]

PIRA, meanwhile, tried to draw maximum propaganda value from the Gazelle crash. It was front page news in the republican newspaper *An Phoblacht* (by contrast, the bombing of the La Mon hotel, which drew widespread condemnation, was barely mentioned) and the South Armagh brigade immediately released a statement claiming responsibility: 'The helicopter was shot down by our 1st Battalion, operating at Jonesborough and using a new type of special magnetic bullet designed for aerial targets and not before used by units.'

Disputing PIRA's claim to have brought down the helicopter, a British Army spokesman also poured scorn on their revelation that 'special magnetic bullets' had been used, pointing out that no such ammunition type existed. 'The tests have not shown any signs of bullet wounds in the bodies or any bullet marks on the helicopter,' Secretary of State for Northern Ireland Roy Mason confirmed three days after the crash.[16]

To counter PIRA's claims, the Army indicated it would publish the findings of the Board of Inquiry set up to investigate the crash. However, they later backtracked and the report remained classified. In December, the Army's chief press officer at HQNI told journalists: 'All that I can say is that Lt Col Corden-Lloyd was killed in a flying accident – I repeat, a flying accident – while engaged in operations over South Armagh.'[17]

The crash report was finally declassified more than thirty years later. While confirming that 'close examination of the wreckage revealed no evidence of a bullet strike on the helicopter', the opinion of the Board was that 'hostile action cannot be dismissed as a contributory cause of the accident and was probably significant'. Sergeant Ives, the report revealed, had only been stationed in Northern Ireland for a week prior to the incident and had never come under fire before.

Although the Board found that there was 'no evidence which indicates positively the precise cause of this accident', they judged that the 'operational stress and threat of hostile action to which Sgt Ives was not accustomed' was a significant factor in the crash. The Board's Convening Officer concluded that the crash 'was largely attributable to the immediate operational pressures and, whilst the aircraft was not shot down, that the PIRA had some grounds for claiming a kill'.[18]

The GOC Northern Ireland at the time, Lieutenant General Sir Timothy Creasey, was in no doubt that the IRA was responsible for the loss of Gazelle XX404. In his closing remarks summarizing the Board's findings, he wrote: 'I consider the crash was a direct result of the terrorist activity in the area.'[19]

A year later the M60 was again used by the South Armagh brigade in a major attack on an Army helicopter.

On 3 March 1979 a Scout was flying over Glasdrumman when one of the passengers, Major Charles Woodrow, commanding a company of 2nd Grenadier Guards, spotted a parked tipper lorry reported stolen earlier that day, which he suspected was about to be used in a mortar attack on a nearby Army watchtower. Just a few days earlier Woodrow had foiled a similar planned attack when the pilot of the Gazelle he was travelling in saw twenty PIRA men preparing a lorry fitted with a mortar baseplate in a field near Crossmaglen. Though heavily outnumbered, Woodrow and another guardsman were landed by the Gazelle and engaged the PIRA gang, forcing them to retreat across the border.

On this occasion, however, it was a set-up. Hidden in three nearby firing positions was an ASU armed with an M60 and assault rifles, with the lorry being used as bait to lure the helicopter into their carefully prepared ambush. 'We were just coming in to have a look, when they opened fire on us – very heavily indeed,' Woodrow recalled.

The IRA fired over a hundred rounds in the attack, hitting the Scout nine times. 'They were firing tracers at us, and one shot set the machine on fire, although we managed to put this out fairly quickly,' he added. Another round shattered the windscreen, cutting the pilot's face with shards of flying Perspex and almost causing him to lose control, while Woodrow himself was hit in the leg. 'I took a crease and two proper shots. The pilot was hurt quite badly, with shrapnel in his face, and a young officer riding in the back was also badly wounded.' Another round hit a rotor blade, 'with the result that the aircraft became very unstable'.

Despite his injuries and the damage to the Scout, the pilot managed to regain control just moments before the helicopter was about to hit the ground and landed safely at Crossmaglen. 'With the pilot in a state of shock, we were lucky, I suppose, to make it back to base,' reflected Major Woodrow.[20]

That year continued to be an eventful one for helicopter crews in South Armagh. On 11 July Gardaí investigating the reported theft of a cabin cruiser on its trailer in Dundalk found the missing boat on Lough Ross, on the border between County Armagh and Monaghan in the Republic. As the cruiser was on the UK side of the lough, they informed the RUC and a helicopter carrying a joint patrol of police and soldiers of the 1st Bn Queen's Own Highlanders was flown to the scene. Upon reaching the lough the pilot found the boat aground and three armed PIRA men racing for the Irish border. 'The patrol was landed and, as the helicopter was taking off, one shot was fired at it. Fire was returned and an armed man was believed to have been hit before escaping into the

Republic,' the new Secretary of State for Northern Ireland, Humphrey Atkins, informed Parliament on 25 July.[21]

Two volunteers were captured, both experienced PIRA bombers, and a search of the stolen cabin cruiser unearthed radio-control equipment. It was thought that PIRA were preparing the vessel for use as a floating bomb, intending to detonate it by radio control on Carlingford Lough and take out the Royal Navy patrol boat based in the lough.[22] The find alerted the security forces to just how sophisticated the Provisional IRA's bombmaking capability had now become. A few weeks later that capability would be demonstrated to devastating effect at Warrenpoint, when similar radio-control equipment was used in the double bomb attack that killed eighteen British soldiers.

The Warrenpoint massacre brought the long-running sore of Anglo-Irish cross-border security co-operation – or rather, as many in the British camp saw it, the lack of it – to a head, as a furious Margaret Thatcher ordered an emergency meeting with Irish Taoiseach Jack Lynch at Downing Street to discuss improving the present arrangements, which was held on 5 September. More detailed discussions took place a month later between Humphrey Atkins and the Irish Foreign Minister Michael O'Kennedy and Justice Minister Gerard Collins.

Top of the agenda was helicopter overflights. Warrenpoint, the British believed, highlighted the need for British helicopters to be permitted to pursue terrorist suspects across the border, as it was thought the bombers had remained in place for some time after detonating the first device before setting off the second bomb. In a memo to the PM, Atkins reported that the meeting had been productive and there was agreement 'that certain border areas, notably South Armagh, needed reinforcing on both sides'. On the question of overflights, the Irish government were 'now ready to permit helicopters to cross the border as a direct follow-up of serious incidents, subject to a number of detailed operational conditions which we were able to accept'. The main stipulation was that military aircraft could penetrate Irish airspace by no more than five kilometres (the British had pressed for ten). The Irish, Atkins wrote, were 'insistent on this since they are highly suspicious of the dangers of abuse, and frightened of the political side-effects of regular appearances of British helicopters in their border areas'.[23]

But this and other concessions secured at the meeting, including allowing direct communication between British helicopter crews and the Garda, failed to impress the PM, who scribbled on the memo: 'I'm afraid this amounts to very little indeed.'

Northern Ireland Office officials, however, were generally satisfied with the outcome of the Anglo-Irish talks and on 10 October wrote to Downing Street to assure the PM that they had 'obtained most of what we wanted' and insisted that 'the Army are entirely happy with the limitation to five kilometres'. It was also agreed that the Irish Air Corps would station one of their Alouette helicopters at Dundalk to help patrol the South Armagh/Monaghan border. 'We shall therefore,' the memo pointed out, 'have joint patrolling by helicopters'.

Overall, the NIO felt that the meetings had 'produced a quite new and substantially higher level of co-operation'.[24] But when news of the secret deal to grant overflight rights to the British was reported in the press in November it sparked an outcry in the Republic. 'We have not given the British Government the right of invading our sovereign territory,' Lynch insisted.[25] That, however, was exactly what his political opponents accused him of doing, and the dispute was a major factor in forcing his resignation the following month.

It would be a long time before the agreements reached over security co-operation would have any real impact on the ground, and in the meantime PIRA attacks on British helicopters continued. At 1100 hours on 10 September 1979, five days after the crunch meeting between Thatcher and Lynch at Downing Street, a Gazelle of 3 CBAS came under Armalite fire as it flew along the border near the village of Cullaville, at a height of 130 feet. The incident report recorded:

> As it was turning it was fired on from a firing point to the south.
> The pilot heard what he thought to be the main rotor splintering.
> The radio went dead and a small electric fire started. Neither the

pilot nor his 3 passengers were injured and the helicopter was able to fly to Crossmaglen.

An examination of the Gazelle after landing found that it had been hit by a single 5.56mm Armalite round, which damaged the radio and cut several cables before becoming lodged in a passenger seat.[26]

On 7 May 1981, amid widespread disorder throughout nationalist areas of the province following the death of PIRA hunger striker Bobby Sands, another Gazelle was hit, close to the scene of the previous attack. The helicopter was flying low over the Concession Road near Cullaville, when six volunteers manning an IVCP opened fire with assault rifles. According to the incident report, 'Three rounds struck the helicopter's rotor blades. Fire was not returned and there were no casualties.'[27]

Between 1974 and 1981 at least thirteen British military aircraft had been hit by PIRA ground fire, but in that period the South Armagh brigade could only claim the destruction of a single helicopter – Lieutenant Colonel Corden-Lloyd's Gazelle at Jonesborough. It had become clear to them that if they were ever to seriously threaten British control of the air in South Armagh more formidable weaponry would be required.

And the leadership of the Provisional IRA was already working on delivering the necessary hardware.

Chapter Six

'If it flies, it dies'
The SAM Threat

In 1979 a top secret British Army report written by Brigadier James Glover of the Defence Intelligence Staff became public after a copy embarrassingly fell into the hands of PIRA. Entitled *Future Terrorist Trends*, the report forecast likely developments in PIRA strategy in Northern Ireland over the coming few years. Among the areas Glover examined was the Provisionals' anti-aircraft campaign. While dismissing PIRA's attempts so far at bringing down helicopters as 'few and ineffective', Glover pointed out in his report that, 'PIRA has long wished to obtain handheld anti-aircraft missiles' and warned that some SAMs 'may well be in their hands before the end of the period [the mid-1980s].'[1]

Brigadier Glover's assessment was accurate. After a decade of war, it had become clear to PIRA that if they were to seriously challenge British control of the air in places like South Armagh they needed more sophisticated weaponry. To this end, in 1981 the Provisional IRA leadership sent one of its top men, 40-year-old Gabriel Megahey from Belfast (known as 'Skinny Legs'), to New York to take over its vital gun-running operation in North America. At the top of Megahey's shopping list were surface-to-air missiles. 'We felt that if we could nullify the helicopter, we would be well on our way to winning the war,' he explained.[2]

With the help of its network of Irish-American supporters, the IRA had acquired many hundreds of guns from the US since the outbreak of the 'Troubles'. Getting hold of shoulder-launched SAMs, however, would be an altogether more challenging proposition.

But in March 1982 there was an apparent breakthrough when one of Megahey's associates told him that an underworld contact, Michael Hanratty – an electronics expert from whom PIRA were negotiating to buy fusing mechanisms for bombs – had assured him that he knew a group of Latin-American arms dealers based in Miami who might have some Redeyes for sale.

The General Dynamics FIM-43 Redeye was a shoulder-launched surface-to-air missile system developed in the 1960s for the US Army and Marine Corps. Designed to be operated by one man, the missile has a maximum range of around 8,500 feet and is guided to its target by an infra-red seeker head, which homes in on the hot gases produced by an aircraft's exhausts. Although vulnerable to anti-missile countermeasures such as flares, which when ejected from the targeted aircraft can decoy the missile away, the Redeye was relatively simple to operate and had proven effective in Nicaragua in the 1980s, where the CIA-backed Contra rebels shot down several army helicopters with the system.

On 2 May Hanratty introduced a member of the IRA arms-smuggling team, Andrew Duggan, an Irish-American construction foreman, to one of the arms dealers, who called himself 'Enrique'. Duggan impressed upon Enrique the importance of SAMs to the IRA, telling him they were a 'number one priority', and arranging a further meeting at a warehouse in New Orleans.

At this point Megahey brought in another PIRA volunteer, Gerry McGeough from County Tyrone, to assist in the negotiations. McGeough, whose grandfather had fought against the British in the Anglo-Irish War, was well aware of the importance of his American mission to PIRA's cause. 'Taking out British Army helicopters would have worked wonders for morale and boosted our ability to prosecute the war on a wider level,' he said. 'It would also have had a corresponding effect on the British, not just operationally but in terms of undermining their morale and weakening their resolve.'[3]

McGeough's confidence in the capability of the Redeye to tip the strategic balance of the war in South Armagh in PIRA's favour was not misplaced. At this point in the conflict British helicopters in Northern Ireland were not fitted with sophisticated anti-missile defences and were thus highly vulnerable to SAMs.

At the New Orleans meeting, McGeough and a PIRA associate successfully negotiated a deal for five Redeyes, at $10,000 apiece, along with several dozen Armalite rifles, to be shipped to Ireland from Port Newark, New Jersey. To satisfy himself that everything was above board, Megahey insisted on meeting personally with one of the Latino arms dealers before any money was handed over. At the meeting, held in a New York hotel room on 11 June 1982, an edgy Megahey expressed his concerns that he could be dealing with an undercover policeman and issued a chilling warning to the arms seller. 'I know one thing for sure – if any of my men get nicked, you're dead'. Despite his suspicions that the deal could be a set-up, the prize of securing SAMs overcame his caution. 'He took the chance because the Redeyes were so important to the IRA given the damage helicopters were doing to operations,' revealed another volunteer.[4]

Ten days later Megahey was leaving a construction site in Manhattan with Duggan when they were suddenly grabbed by a squad of FBI agents in plainclothes who, recalled Megahey, pointed 'a barrage of guns' at him. A similar swoop was being carried out simultaneously in Brooklyn where two more men involved in the plot, brothers Eamon and Colm Meehan, were arrested.

Megahey and his associates had been the victims of an elaborate FBI sting; 'Enrique' and the other arms dealers they had been negotiating with were in fact undercover Federal agents, members of an elite unit set up two years before, which was tasked specifically with smashing the Provisionals' gun-running network in the US. The FBI operation had been set in motion in May 1981, when PIRA had first made contact with Hanratty, who was working as an FBI informant. Having secretly recorded all their meetings with the PIRA men and tapped their phone conversations, the FBI had all the evidence they needed.

A small consignment of arms (minus the Redeyes) in two crates marked as containing roller skates was allowed to set sail from Port Newark, bound for Limerick, where the Garda, tipped off by the FBI, arrested two more PIRA men waiting to take delivery of the weapons. Only McGeough slipped through the FBI's fingers, escaping back to Ireland (he was eventually captured in the Netherlands in 1988, extradited to the US and sentenced to three years for his part in the arms-smuggling plot).

After a trial at the US District Court in Brooklyn lasting nine weeks, on 13 May 1983 Gabriel Megahey, the Meehan brothers and Duggan were found guilty of plotting to smuggle weapons to PIRA. Megahey was sentenced to seven years, while Duggan and Eamon Meehan each received three years and Colm Meehan two years imprisonment. It was the most successful prosecution of PIRA members in the US so far, where convictions of IRA suspects had traditionally been difficult to secure.

The FBI and the British authorities were jubilant. Yet even as they celebrated their success in smashing the Megahey gun-running network and thwarting PIRA's efforts to obtain Redeyes, the South Armagh brigade was preparing its next strike.

'Clearly a well planned and executed attack'

For the British Army, 20 July 1982 was one of the blackest days in the long, bloody history of the 'Troubles'. At 1040 hours, in London's Hyde Park four soldiers of the Blues and Royals were killed by a PIRA bomb during the Changing the Guard ceremony, along with seven of their horses. Little more than two hours later the terrorists struck again with a second bomb, this time at the bandstand in Regents Park. A further seven bandsmen of the Royal Green Jackets were massacred here.

But the IRA wasn't finished yet. With the Army reeling from the double attack in London, in South Armagh PIRA was determined to inflict yet more casualties on the British military. The third target of the day was a Wessex (serial XR506) on a routine flight from Forkhill to Bessbrook Mill, carrying nine soldiers and three crew.

Just after 1630 hours, as the helicopter passed Croslieve Hill, around eight miles from Bessbrook, a PIRA ambush team opened up with multiple automatic weapons, including Armalites, an M60 and a Browning M2 heavy machine gun, from four firing points at the foot of the hill.

According to the Army incident report, some of those on board the Wessex 'heard crackling sounds', but the crew were unaware of having come under fire until after landing at Bessbrook Mill ten minutes later, where they found 'nine holes spread along the whole length of the fuselage'.[5]

The subsequent investigation estimated that the PIRA ambush team consisted of up to fifteen gunmen, who had been lying in wait for a suitable target for several hours, concealed from the air under camouflage netting, and had fired a total of 103 rounds at the Wessex when it came within range. However, only two of those rounds came from the most potent weapon they employed that afternoon: the Browning M2 .50 calibre heavy machine gun.

Designed by the American gunmaker John Browning during the First World War, the famous 'Fifty Cal', as it is popularly known, is one of the world's most formidable HMGs, firing a bullet a half-an-inch in diameter. It's believed PIRA managed to smuggle at least two of these weapons into Ireland from the US during the late 1970s, with the attack on the Wessex in July 1982 being one of the first times it was used in Northern Ireland. But on that occasion the weapon jammed almost as soon as the operator opened fire, almost certainly due to the age of the ammunition, which date stamps found on the spent cartridge cases by the security forces at the firing point revealed had been manufactured in 1943.

In his report on the attack, the SHFNI's CO, Wing Commander Nicholson, stated that the crew had had 'a narrow escape', while the Army's investigation found that the South Armagh brigade had been able to anticipate the Wessex flight because a predictable flight pattern had been set on the route between Forkhill and Bessbrook. 'From the use of such prestige weapons and the number of firers involved, it seems that PIRA had not only identified this pattern but were saving the shoot as part of a spectacular to coincide with the London bombings.' The report also judged that it was 'clearly a well planned and executed attack which fortunately failed to achieve its spectacular objective', and noted that 'the meticulous planning and execution of the shoot point to high-level, experienced terrorists'.[6]

Less than three weeks later, on the night of 9 August, another Wessex was hit when it came under small-arms fire near the Kilnasaggart bridge, four miles from the previous month's attack, as it came in to land. 'The captain reacted well when the tracer was spotted and the aircraft was only hit once,' the Operations Record Book noted. The master air loadmaster was nicked by a shrapnel fragment after a single 5.56mm round hit the cabin door, which was 'disconcerting but fortunately not more serious'.[7]

While neither attack had been successful, the security forces realized they could ill afford to be complacent. As the report into the 20 July shooting gloomily pointed out: 'The fact remains that both the M60 and the .50 are still around and there can be little doubt that another helicopter shoot will be staged.'[8]

That shoot came less than a year later, in what the newly appointed CO of 72 Squadron, Wing Commander Day, described as 'potentially the most lethal attack against SH [Support Helicopters] since NI operations began in 1969'.[9]

The target was again XR506, the same Wessex the South Armagh brigade damaged on 20 July 1982. Shortly after 1900 hours on 12 May 1983, the day before Gabriel Megahey and his accomplices were convicted in the SAM-smuggling plot, XR506's pilot, a squadron leader, was flying a seven-strong squad of Royal Marines from Crossmaglen to Bessbrook when, as he was approaching the village of Silverbridge, 'I heard rapid gunfire followed very soon after by bullets hitting the aircraft on the front and port side. The co-pilot's windscreen shattered and he was hit by shrapnel.'[10]

He immediately banked sharply to the right, dropped down to fifty feet and increased speed, with the intense barrage of fire continuing for another twenty seconds. Once clear of the danger zone, the pilot and his crew assessed the damage. His co-pilot had been wounded in the shoulder and was bleeding heavily, while one of the marines in the main cabin had also been hit, though his flak-jacket saved him from serious injury.

Radioing a mayday call, the squadron leader flew on towards Bessbrook Mill. But it quickly became apparent that the Wessex had sustained more serious damage in the attack than first thought. The port engine had been hit and was losing oil pressure, as had the aft fuel tanks, one of which was leaking fuel at an alarming rate. By cross-feeding fuel from the other tanks the pilot succeeded in keeping the helicopter airborne and landed at Bessbrook seven minutes later, where his injured co-pilot was rushed to Belfast's Musgrave Park Hospital.

For saving the Wessex, the pilot was Mentioned in Despatches. 'In spite of the extensive damage to his aircraft, the captain made a copy book recovery to Bessbrook,' noted the Squadron Operations Record Book, which went on to state that 'the performance of the entire crew was exemplary'.

The subsequent investigation discovered that the PIRA team had fired a total of 274 rounds from six firing points, twenty-three of which struck XR506, damaging the port engine, the hydraulics, one of the main rotor blades and holing the fuel tanks. Among the weapons used was the Browning .50 HMG which, noted Wing Commander Day, 'operated quite well for the first time and managed to fire some 18 rounds of link'.

As with the attack on 20 July 1982 the gunmen had probably remained in position for several hours, while Day pointed out that the site of the ambush had been carefully selected so that 'an approaching helicopter, even at low level, could be seen for some distance'. What set this attack apart from previous ones, however, was PIRA's 'preparedness to set up such a large ambush a relatively long way from the border'.[11]

The close call led to a review of flying tactics in South Armagh. The question of arming helicopters was re-examined, but again ruled out due to the difficulty of positively identifying targets on the ground and obtaining any degree of accuracy with a GPMG from a moving helicopter. Instead, communications security was tightened in case PIRA were listening in to military radio traffic, restrictions on pilots flying lower than 100 feet were relaxed, which would offer enemy gunmen less time to bring their weapons to bear on the target, and the importance of taking indirect routes when flying between bases was emphasized.

However, as Wing Commander Day observed, there was no surefire counter to the threat posed by PIRA. 'The intensity of helicopter operations in South Armagh makes the probability of a re-attack very high,' he conceded.[12]

Two years would pass before that re-attack took place. Once again the target was a 72 Squadron Wessex, and in a sign of how bold the South

Armagh brigade was becoming it took place in the heart of Crossmaglen, close to the security forces base. For this attack, PIRA also introduced a new tactic: using their Browning .50s mounted on the back of a flatbed lorry, hidden beneath a tarpaulin.

On the afternoon of 24 May 1985 the lorry was parked on the Dundalk Road, along with a back-up car containing five volunteers. At 1430 hours, as the Wessex came in to land at the Crossmaglen base, the tarpaulin was hauled off to reveal two masked volunteers manning a pair of Brownings, who opened fire with a sustained burst. The helicopter was hit three times – in the cab, engine intake and tail – but there were no injuries. A soldier on guard duty at the base returned fire at the lorry but claimed no hits. The lorry then sped off south-east along the Dundalk Road, the gunmen continuing to fire, before escaping across the border.[13]

As in the previous attacks, the crew had good reason to be grateful for the robustness of the sturdy Westland machine, for despite the damage inflicted it remained airborne. The pilot diverted to Bessbrook where he made a safe landing.

It had been another well-planned and carefully prepared ambush. PIRA had used its network of 'dickers' throughout the town to track the movements of the company of 1st King's Own Scottish Borderers stationed in Crossmaglen, waiting until most of the unit's patrols were off the streets before launching the attack. The major commanding the KOSB company admitted to being impressed by the audacity of the ambush: 'That was a bold attack …. They produced premium weapons, high visibility weapons, in an attempt to shoot down a high visibility target, a helicopter.'[14]

Yet the fact remained that, sixteen years after the conflict began, the British had only lost a single helicopter as a result of IRA action. The repeated failures to add to this tally prompted the Provisionals to renew their efforts to purchase surface-to-air missiles on the black market. And they now set their sights on acquiring the most deadly SAM of all.

Armed with a four-barrelled rotary cannon in the nose capable of firing 4,000 rounds per minute and rocket pods mounted on its stub wings, the Mi-24 'Hind' is a truly fearsome helicopter gunship. To the Afghan mujahedeen, who often found themselves on the receiving end of its dev-astating firepower, it was known as Satan's Chariot. During their war against the occupying Soviet forces in Afghanistan in the 1980s the muja-hedeen often tried to shoot down these aircraft, but thanks to their thick armour they enjoyed only limited success.

Until 25 September 1986. On that day three of the dreaded Hinds were shot down in rapid succession as they came in to land at Jalalabad air base in eastern Afghanistan. All three had fallen victim to a new weapon supplied to the guerrillas by the CIA – the Stinger shoulder-launched surface-to-air missile.[15]

Introduced into US Army service in 1981, the General Dynamics FIM-92 Stinger was a major improvement on all other MANPADS of the period. Requiring little training to use, it can lock on to a target from any angle and has a considerably greater range than its predecessor, the Redeye, or its Russian equivalent, the SA-7 'Strela', being capable of hitting an aircraft up to an altitude of 12,500 feet. But its most import-ant advance was in the missile's guidance system, which was far more resistant to anti-missile countermeasures like flares, greatly increasing the likelihood of a 'kill'. As the US military were fond of saying of the Stinger: 'If it flies, it dies'.[16]

The weapon was first used in action by the SAS in the Falklands war, where it brought down an Argentine Pucará ground-attack aircraft on 21 May 1982, followed by a Puma helicopter nine days later. But it was during the Soviet-Afghan War that the Stinger really established its rep-utation for deadly efficiency.

By 1986, the seventh year of the Soviet occupation of Afghanistan, the mujahedeen guerrillas were on the back foot, under severe pressure from Soviet airpower, not least in the form of the Mi-24 Hind. Soon after the Soviet invasion in 1979 the CIA began supporting the guerril-las through Operation CYCLONE, a covert programme of training and arms supplies channelled through Pakistan. In the mid-1980s, fearing that the mujahedeen were on the brink of defeat, the CIA stepped up their support by supplying hundreds of Stingers to the guerrillas, after overcoming opposition from some in Washington who were nervous of handing over such an advanced piece of military hardware to an unpredictable guerrilla army, over which they had little control, and fearful that some would inevitably fall into Russian hands.

After its impressive debut on the Afghan battlefield in September 1986, for the remainder of the war the Stinger went on to take a heavy toll of Soviet aircraft, especially helicopters. After the war a CIA analysis claimed that the missile enjoyed a 70 per cent success rate with the mujahedeen, downing 269 aircraft – well over half of all Soviet losses in the war. Some of those involved in Operation CYCLONE even credited the Stinger with being the single most important factor in persuading Moscow to quit Afghanistan in February 1989.[17]

While these claims have been disputed by other sources, who insist the Stinger's kill rate was exaggerated by the CIA, there's little doubt that the missile was greatly feared by Soviet pilots. According to Brigadier Mohammed Yousaf of Pakistan's ISI intelligence service, who co-ordinated US arms supplies to the mujahedeen during the war, 'after we started using Stingers, all helicopter pilots began to show a marked disinclination to press home attacks'.[18]

With the introduction of the Stinger, Soviet air crews were forced to fly extremely low, using the mountainous terrain to mask their movements, though this in turn made them more vulnerable to attack from heavy machine guns and RPGs. So desperate were the Russians to unlock the Stinger's secrets that the Soviet defence minister promised that the first soldier to capture an intact example would immediately be made a Hero of the Soviet Union.[19]

Along with the CIA and defence analysts, also taking a close interest in the Stinger's success in Afghanistan was the Provisional IRA. This, clearly, was the wonder weapon they had long been searching for to cancel out the crucial British advantage of air mobility in South Armagh, and they became determined to lay their hands on one.

Sale of the century

An opportunity to obtain a Stinger appeared to present itself in 1989 when Kevin McKinley, a PIRA suspect from Belfast who was based in

Florida, was introduced through a local firearms enthusiast to two arms dealers, L.J. Connelly, who claimed to be an Irish-American with IRA sympathies, and his friend Greg. At a meeting at a Florida bar on 20 November 1989 McKinley negotiated a deal to buy detonators, .50 calibre sniper rifles and ammunition. But what he really wanted was a Stinger, as he made clear to the two men during their conversation. 'Can you get a Stinger?' he enquired. 'That's number one on our list.' The arms dealers assured him they could, and that the price would be $50,000. As the going rate for a black market Stinger was around three times that figure, McKinley later said he thought this was 'the sale of the century'.[20]

But once again PIRA was being drawn into another 'sting'. 'LJ' and 'Greg' were in fact undercover Federal agents Lawrence O'Donnell and John Fields, who were part of a joint operation between the FBI and the Bureau of Alcohol, Tobacco and Firearms, and every word of their conversation with McKinley was being secretly recorded.

At another meeting a few weeks later McKinley emphasized the importance of the Stinger to PIRA in South Armagh. 'This is for a chopper ... the Brits, they can't come in, they can't drive because of landmines ... the only way they can come in is by air. We beat them in the air so they can't come back,' he told the undercover agents.[21] McKinley also assured the two men the weapon would only be used against the British in Northern Ireland, to assuage their fears that US citizens might be killed by the missile.

Meanwhile, another Provisional IRA suspect, Seamus Moley, spent the next few weeks trying to raise the cash for the deal, which wiretaps of McKinley's phone conversations revealed was proving difficult, forcing the two men to keep stalling on the deal. Finally, in early January the money was in place and McKinley handed over a down payment of $2,500 to 'LJ' and 'Greg', with the balance of $47,500 to be paid on delivery of the missile.

As the deal edged towards its conclusion, an alleged PIRA weapons expert, Joseph McColgan, arrived in Florida from Belfast to authenticate the Stinger. On 12 January 1990 he met 'LJ' and 'Greg' in a warehouse in West Palm Beach County, Florida, where they handed him a (de-activated) Stinger the US Marine Corps had lent to the FBI. 'LJ' showed the Irishman how to operate the missile and, satisfied that all was well and that PIRA had now finally acquired a war-winning weapon, he placed it on the back seat of his hire car, hidden beneath a blanket.

As he was about to drive off with the missile, more agents hiding nearby made their move, arresting McColgan, followed by McKinley and Moley shortly afterwards. Charged with conspiring to unlawfully export a Stinger missile, during their month-long trial held at the US District Court in Fort Lauderdale McKinley admitted his aim was to buy a Stinger and told the court how important the weapon was to PIRA: 'I genuinely believed that if we got something like that, it could change the course of what was happening in Northern Ireland.'[22] Found guilty on 11 December 1990, McKinley and his co-defendants were each sentenced to four years.

Following on from the arrest of Gabriel Megahey in 1982, and the uncovering of another plot to smuggle Redeyes from the US to Ireland in 1986, which led to the capture of two more PIRA members in Boston, the so-called 'Stinger sting' was a major success for US law enforcement. After the verdict was delivered, Robert Creighton of the Bureau of Alcohol, Tobacco and Firearms declared: 'This strikes a significant blow against Irish Republican Army operations within the United States.'[23]

The exposure of PIRA's attempts to acquire SAMs in America brought home to aircrews serving in Northern Ireland the threat of terrorists equipped with guided missiles, leading to a rethink on flying tactics. 'We had to fly accordingly, particularly in South Armagh,' said Royal Navy pilot Michael Booth. 'We had to fly very low. We wouldn't fly at high level, unless you really needed to.'[24]

Visiting VIPs gained first-hand experience of the 'nap-of-the-earth' tactics pilots now employed, including the then Prime Minister Margaret Thatcher. As PIRA's number one target in the 1980s, enormous security precautions were put in place to protect her from SAMs whenever she visited the province. The helicopter carrying her would always fly at tree-top level, carry a door gunner manning a GPMG and be escorted by a second helicopter, believed to be fitted out with the latest ECM equipment to jam any guided missile. After enduring one such ultra-low-level flight to a security forces base in County Fermanagh, her press secretary Bernard Ingham quipped to a journalist travelling in the Wessex with them: 'That's the first time I've ever flown underground. Even the cows ducked!'[25]

In March 1988 it was also disclosed that the helicopter fleet in Northern Ireland had been fitted with the AN/ALQ-144 IRCM (Infra-Red Counter Measures) pod. Developed in the 1970s in response to aircraft losses suffered by the US military to the Soviet SA-7 'Strela' in the closing stages of the Vietnam war, this device redirects the infra-red energy that a heat-seeking SAM homes in on away from the target aircraft, hopefully deflecting the missile off course. It was more effective than the standard counter-measure, flares ejected from the aircraft to confuse the seeker-head, as only a limited supply of these could be carried and they had to be deployed at the right time by the crew. Further protection was provided by the fitting of 'baffles', a suppressor system which reduces the infra-red heat signature of a helicopter by mixing cooler air into the hot gases emitted by the engines, making it more difficult for the SAM operator to gain a lock.

But even while the IRA's attempts at securing Redeyes and Stingers in the US were being repeatedly thwarted by the FBI, another source of arms supply was opening up in the mid-1980s, one which would finally provide the Provisionals with the arsenal they needed to bring down helicopters, including the much sought-after SAMs.

Chapter Seven

Gifts from the Colonel

For the crew of Lynx XZ664 the flight from Crossmaglen to Bessbrook Mill on 23 June 1988 was expected to be just another routine hop between SF bases. But at 1255 hours, as they were approaching Aughanduff Upper Mountain, a 234-metre high hill around five kilometres from the village of Silverbridge, several heavy calibre rounds slammed into the tail boom and rotors, easily tearing through the metal. One of the Gem turboshaft engines cut out and the Lynx went into a spin. Lieutenant David Richardson, a Royal Navy pilot who was serving on attachment with the AAC's 665 Squadron, radioed a mayday while fighting desperately with the controls, trying to keep the helicopter in the air. But the damage was too severe and the Lynx came down hard in a field near Cashel Lough, slightly injuring one of the crew.

But the danger hadn't yet passed. Armed with AK-47 assault rifles and an RPG-7, the twelve-strong PIRA unit that had brought down the helicopter from their positions on Aughanduff mountain now went in search of the crash site, determined to destroy the Lynx and finish off its three-man crew and the two passengers they were carrying. Fortunately, the arrival of the ARF in another Lynx scrambled from Bessbrook the moment Richardson had radioed his mayday forced the attackers to withdraw before completing the job. For his skill in bringing down the crippled helicopter without serious injury to crew or passengers, Lieutenant Richardson was later awarded a Queen's Commendation for Valuable Service in the Air.

In their statement claiming responsibility for the attack PIRA revealed that they had used AK-47s, three GPMGs and two heavy machine guns firing armour-piercing ammunition to shoot down the helicopter. This was confirmed by Army ballistics experts, whose examination of the damaged helicopter found that XZ664 had been hit by a total of fifteen rounds, several of which came from a DShK heavy machine gun, the first time such a weapon had been used by PIRA.

Designed by the Soviet engineers Vasily Degtyarov and Georgi Shpagin, the DShK was a Russian machine gun of 12.7mm calibre, which became the Red Army's standard HMG after entering service in 1939, and remains in widespread use to this day. Nicknamed the Dushka (Russian for 'Sweetheart'), it can punch through 15mm-thick armour at 500 metres and has an effective range of over a kilometre. 'They were real brutes,' said one PIRA volunteer. 'The firepower was devastating.'[1] But though possessing fearsome hitting power, the Dushka is a heavy and cumbersome weapon, requiring three men to carry and set up, and has a relatively slow rate of fire. Nevertheless, the introduction of this formidable HMG in South Armagh greatly boosted PIRA's ability to prosecute attacks on helicopters.

The first loss of a military aircraft directly attributable to hostile fire since Operation BANNER commenced nineteen years before was a cause of grave concern to the British. A week after the shooting down of XZ664, Secretary of State for Northern Ireland Tom King admitted in Parliament that, 'Any development of a threat to helicopters would be a serious matter and involve alterations to the operating practices of the security forces'.[2] After this attack, pilots serving in South Armagh began carrying a Heckler & Koch HK53 assault rifle in the cockpit, in addition to their Browning 9mm pistols, in case they were forced down and had to defend themselves against a PIRA follow-up.

For PIRA the successful downing of the Lynx came as a major morale boost at a time when their campaign was faltering. At the north Armagh village of Loughgall in May 1987 eight volunteers from the East Tyrone brigade were wiped out in an SAS ambush whilst attacking an RUC station, and in February 1988 two of the South Armagh brigade's top bombmakers, Brendan Moley and Brendan Burns (who was suspected of carrying out the Warrenpoint attack), were killed in an 'own-goal' explosion at the village of Creggan near Crossmaglen when a bomb they were loading into a van went off prematurely. Security forces casualties in South Armagh had also dwindled, with only a single British soldier being killed in the region in the eighteen months prior to the shooting down of the Lynx.

One of the main reasons for this sharp reduction in casualties was the establishment of a chain of twelve heavily fortified watchtowers, known as 'Romeo' and 'Golf' towers, ringing South Armagh, the construction of which began in the mid-1980s under the codenames Operations ENTIRETY and MAGISTRATE. Sited on the high ground, these multi-million pound installations, bristling with an array of sophisticated surveillance equipment and each housing up to thirty soldiers, allowed the Army to dominate the South Armagh countryside, severely restricting the freedom of movement PIRA had previously enjoyed.

Determined to maximise the propaganda value of the Lynx shootdown, the PIRA ambush team had even brought along a video camera to record the historic moment when they finally succeeded in bringing down a British helicopter. Unfortunately for PIRA's propaganda department, the cameraman failed to capture the actual crash of the Lynx, pointing his camera instead at the masked volunteers opening up with their machine guns. According to the Irish journalist and IRA expert Ed Moloney, Sinn Fein's director of publicity was 'fuming at the cameraman' after viewing the footage.[3] Instead, republicans commemorated the shooting down of the helicopter in a mural painted on the wall of Sinn Fein's offices in west Belfast.

The Dushka heavy machine guns used in the attack were supplied to PIRA by their long-time benefactor, Colonel Muammar Gaddafi. The relationship between the Provisionals and the unstable Libyan dictator stretched back to the early days of the 'Troubles'. Amid deteriorating relations between London and Tripoli, Gaddafi publicly declared his support for what he described as 'the revolutionaries of Ireland' in a radio broadcast in June 1972.

But Gaddafi's first major arms shipment to the IRA fell into the hands of the Irish authorities when the ship carrying the weapons, the *Claudia*, was intercepted off the County Waterford coast in March 1973 by an Irish Navy patrol vessel after being tracked on its journey from the Mediterranean to Ireland by an RAF Nimrod. The Colonel's interest in the Provisionals then appeared to wane, until it was revived in the 1980s when Anglo-Libyan relations sank to an all-time low following the killing of PC Yvonne Fletcher, who was shot outside the Libyan embassy in London by a gunman firing from inside the building. Once again, Gaddafi telegraphed his renewed support for the IRA in a broadcast on Libyan state radio in April 1984, announcing that he would form an alliance with PIRA, who he insisted were 'liberating the Irish nation from the tyranny of British colonialism'.[4]

With the FBI clamping down on their arms-smuggling activities in the US, Gaddafi's offer of huge quantities of powerful, modern weaponry, free of charge, couldn't have come at a more opportune time for PIRA. On the night of 24 August 1985 the elderly fishing boat *Casamara* brought in the first shipment, containing seven tonnes of arms and ammunition, which was offloaded at Clogga Strand in County Wicklow. Two months later another cargo, this time of ten tonnes, was landed at the same place, again shipped to Ireland from Libya onboard the *Casamara*, which had now been renamed *Kula* in an effort to throw off any Intelligence agencies that might be tracking her.

After Margaret Thatcher allowed British air bases to be used in Operation EL DORADO CANYON, an American attempt to kill Gaddafi in April 1986 with an F-111 air strike on his compound in Tripoli, he responded by stepping up aid to PIRA. In July he sent over a further fourteen tonnes and then in October a massive shipment of eighty tonnes was brought in to Ireland on the *Villa*, a former oil rig replenishment vessel which was twice the size of the *Kula*. Included in these cargoes was the hardware PIRA needed to seriously threaten British air operations in South Armagh, such as DShK heavy machine guns and the shoulder-launched SAMs the Provisionals had long been seeking.

These were SA-7 Strelas (meaning 'Arrow'), Russia's answer to the US Redeye. Given the NATO reporting name 'Grail', the SA-7 has a maximum range of around 7,500 feet and, like the Redeye, is guided by infra-red. The world's most widely used MANPAD system, its first recorded 'kill' came in August 1969 when an Egyptian soldier used one to bring down an Israeli A-4 Skyhawk near the Suez Canal, and it's been used in virtually every significant conflict since.

The epic arms-smuggling operation finally came to an end in November 1987 when the MV *Eksund*, carrying the fifth and, at 150 tonnes, largest arms shipment, was intercepted by the French coastguard off the coast of Brittany. But by then more than 110 tonnes of weapons, ammunition and explosives had been safely landed, including an estimated 650 AK-47 and AKM assault rifles, several tonnes of Semtex explosives, forty General Purpose Machine Guns, twenty RPG-7s, between four and ten SA-7s and around two dozen Dushkas, though according to some sources not all were in full working order.[5] Still, thanks to Gaddafi's largesse, PIRA were now more heavily armed than at any time in their history. A hand-picked group of volunteers, several from the South Armagh brigade, also travelled to Libya during 1986 to receive training on the weapons.

Extending 'Bandit Country'

With their network of secret underground bunkers throughout Ireland crammed with Libyan ordnance, hardliners in PIRA were now in a position to implement a long-cherished plan to intensify their armed campaign and create so-called 'liberated' or 'free zones' along the border, forcing the Army and RUC to abandon their border bases, and effectively extend Bandit Country so that it stretched from South Armagh through County Tyrone and into County Fermanagh. According to Sean O'Callaghan, a senior figure in PIRA's Southern Command who became a Garda informer, the plan was the brainchild of Kevin McKenna, Chief of Staff of PIRA in the 1980s.[6]

Key to the success of the plan was to paralyze British mobility in the border regions by inflicting such losses in the air that the Army would be forced to ground its helicopter fleet.

While the IED problem in Tyrone and Fermanagh was never as severe as in South Armagh, by the late 1980s the security forces had become heavily reliant on air transport in the rural areas of these two counties. The dependence on air travel became more pronounced after a bus carrying soldiers of the 1st Bn Light Infantry, who were returning from leave to their barracks in Omagh, was ripped apart by a large roadside IED close to the County Tyrone town of Ballygawley on 20 August 1988, killing eight soldiers and injuring twenty-eight others. The deadly attack had been carried out, using Libyan-supplied Semtex explosives, by PIRA's East Tyrone brigade, who were considered by security forces chiefs to be second only to their compatriots in South Armagh for ruthless efficiency.

But it wasn't until 11 February 1990 that the East Tyrone brigade finally joined the offensive against British helicopters. That afternoon a Gazelle of 655 Squadron (serial ZB687), flown by a Royal Marine pilot on attachment to the Army Air Corps and carrying three soldiers of the 1st Bn King's Own Scottish Borderers, was providing top cover for a joint RUC/Army patrol investigating suspicious vehicle activity at a border crossing point near Clogher in County Tyrone. By this point in the 'Troubles', Gazelles were frequently used in this role, scouting ahead to alert the 'bricks' on the ground to potential ambush sites, suspect vehicles or possible IEDs. On this occasion, however, the helicopter itself was the target; the alert at the border crossing almost certainly a 'come-on', intended to lure the Gazelle into an ambush.

At around 1630 hours a five-man ASU opened fire with a GPMG and AK-47s. A single 7.62mm round hit the oil-feed pipe, causing the engine to fail, and the helicopter crashed in a field between Augher and Derrygorry, on the border. The pilot, who was later Mentioned in Despatches, and a sergeant major of the KOSB suffered spinal injuries in the crash and the Gazelle was so badly damaged it had to be scrapped.

Jubilant, the East Tyrone brigade swiftly released a statement claiming responsibility: 'Our ASU fired approximately 300 rounds .... This latest attack demonstrates our resourcefulness and ability to strike at the British forces at will.'[7]

Meanwhile, the South Armagh brigade resumed helicopter attacks on 25 September 1990. Late that night a Lynx landed outside the Newtownhamilton base to drop off a load of rations when an ASU opened up with two light machine guns and a Dushka, mounted on a 4 x 4 pick-up truck. As green tracer rounds flashed by, the Lynx immediately took off again and soldiers of the 1st Bn Cheshire Regiment who were help-ing unload the helicopter dived for cover, one being slightly wounded. However, the Lynx was unscathed. 'Everybody was lucky that night for some bizarre reason,' remarked one of the Cheshires present during the attack. 'If the chopper had been hit it would have been a proper disaster.'[8]

Escalation

As a new year dawned, and with media attention focused on events unfolding in the Middle East as Operation DESERT STORM got underway in the Persian Gulf, PIRA dramatically stepped up the pres-sure. At 1922 hours on 31 January 1991 a Wessex carrying several soldiers was lifting off from the Forkhill base when 'it came under a 15-20 sec burst of automatic gunfire from two weapons situated to the west of the SF base'. Spotting the incoming tracer fire, the pilot flew away from the danger zone at low level.[9] The follow-up investigation found that a total of eighty-nine rounds had been fired from a Dushka and a GPMG, again mounted on a pick-up, at a range of around 500 metres. One round hit the Wessex, on the port side of the fuselage, causing only slight damage and no casualties. But the South Armagh brigade's next attack, just two weeks later, met with greater success.

At 1519 hours on 13 February, Lynx ZE380 of 665 Squadron, flying at around 500 feet, was ferrying rations in an underslung load into the Crossmaglen base when the pilot, as he later reported, 'noticed a flash in front of the cockpit followed almost immediately by the sound of strikes hitting the aircraft on the port side behind the cockpit area'. The heli-copter was then 'hit by two further bursts of automatic fire, some rounds striking the cockpit area'. The pilot continued: 'I had the clear impres-sion that we had been engaged by two weapons. The first had a high rate of fire with an associated "cracking" noise. The second a slower rate associated with a "thumping" noise'.[10]

The Lynx had been struck by eight rounds from a Dushka and two more from a GPMG, hitting the main rotor blade, belly panel, cabin roof, main rotor gearbox, avionics loom and cyclic control rod. Follow-up searches led to the recovery of twenty-eight 12.7mm and 174 7.62mm spent cartridge cases at the firing point, which was behind Crossmaglen's community centre.

Occupying the left-hand seat, the aircraft commander, a lieutenant colonel, jettisoned the underslung load and, as the pilot's controls were proving unresponsive, took over control of the bullet-riddled helicopter. 'With the USL released there was sufficient power to pull away,' he explained.

But with the crew continuing to suffer severe control problems due to bullet damage to the cyclic control rod, it was decided to make an emergency landing once out of the immediate danger zone. Finding a suitable field near Silverbridge three kilometres away, the crew carried out a successful 'roll-on' landing. None of the three-man crew was injured in the attack or during the emergency landing.

Now stranded in the heart of Bandit Country, the pilot requested that a second Lynx which had been providing mutual support throughout the emergency return to Bessbrook to pick up an ARF while he and his crew remained at the crash site to protect their helicopter

> since I was concerned that with 2 farm complexes in the immediate vicinity to the field it would be all too easy for an unfriendly 'local' to finish the job PIRA had started. With a GPMG with 400 rounds and 2 x HK 53, each with 2 magazines, I considered we were well able to look after ourselves, and the aircraft.[11]

Fortunately, there was no attempt by PIRA or their supporters to follow up the attack and destroy the helicopter on the ground, although one of the crewmen commented that 'it was a very, very long 10 minutes before the ARF did arrive!'

The Dushka had once again proven itself to be a highly effective weapon in the anti-aircraft role, and the Lynx crew were extremely lucky to avoid serious injury, as the Board of Inquiry report into the attack acknowledged: 'In the case of the 12.7mm rounds a variation of only a few inches would have caused catastrophic damage to vulnerable vital components or killed any passengers in the cabin area', and noted with concern that the terrorists were 'able to acquire and engage the target with comparative ease'.

The Board also 'congratulated the crew on their handling of the aircraft whilst under fire and on their subsequent actions in recovering a damaged aircraft to a safe area'.[12] After being airlifted to Aldergrove by RAF Chinook, where the damage was assessed as Category 4, ZE380 was repaired and soon returned to service.

Thanks to a pilot's skilful actions, PIRA were denied a repeat of their success just two days later. On the evening of 15 February a pair of Lynx were coming in to land near Clogher on the Tyrone/Monaghan border, close to where Gazelle ZB687 had been shot down by the East Tyrone brigade a year earlier, to pick up a patrol from the 1st Bn Duke of Edinburgh's Royal Regiment when one of the Lynx came under sustained fire from terrorists armed with GPMGs. 'Fortunately,' revealed the incident report, 'the aircraft was not hit, and the pilot took instant evasive action, aborting the landing and using the tremendous agility of the helicopter to extricate the aircraft from the situation.'

The pilot flew along the border, trying to locate the firing position, when the terrorists opened fire a second time. 'Again, the pilot was forced to take evasive action,' stated the report. Fearing that the Lynx had been hit, he finally broke off the pursuit. 'His fears', it continued, 'were fortunately unfounded – and not wanting to risk his aircraft further he returned to base.' The Army's report into the attack praised the pilot's actions: 'Although the operation had been well planned and executed in a determined fashion by the terrorist, the pilot through skilful flying and quick reactions averted a much more serious incident.'[13]

A follow-up search of the area by the DERR patrol uncovered a total of 360 spent cartridge cases, along with an empty ammunition box. In a statement the East Tyrone brigade admitted carrying out the attack and claimed to have hit the helicopter, although the RUC insisted that after careful examination of the Lynx upon its return to base 'no strike marks were found'.

Two weeks later, in an attack which bore similarities to that against the RAF Wessex on 24 May 1985, volunteers of the South Armagh brigade

rode into the heart of Crossmaglen in a pick-up truck with an improvised turret mounted atop, stopping just fifty metres from the RUC/
Army base. The turret housed a Dushka heavy machine gun and the
ensuing attack on a pair of Lynx flying overhead was captured on camera
by a TV crew from the Irish state broadcaster RTE, who happened to be
filming a news report in Crossmaglen at the time on allegations of British
Army harassment of civilians in South Armagh. Neither helicopter was
hit during the 30-second attack and the ASU escaped before the troops
in the base could react.

Alarmed by the increasing frequency and boldness of attacks on helicopters in the border areas, British commanders responded by ordering that a
co-pilot be carried on all flights, to take control in the event of the pilot being
incapacitated by ground fire, while re-supply flights to bases in the vulnerable border areas were increasingly flown during the hours of darkness.

In an interview in *An Phoblacht* in February 1991 a PIRA spokesman
boasted that in South Armagh 'the British have been forced onto hilltops
and into the air'. He went on: 'if the IRA increases its capability to take
out choppers' the infrastructure of the security forces could be 'placed in
danger of collapse in these border areas'.[14]

A month later at a republican rally in Crossmaglen to mark the sev-
enty-fifth anniversary of the 1916 Easter rebellion, a masked PIRA volunteer, referring to the fact that it was now routine for two armed Lynx
to be used to escort transport helicopters into the town's base, promised
the cheering crowd that soon the British would require 'five or six helicopters to bring in the rations'.[15] Following the 15 February attack in
County Tyrone, a British Army report admitted: 'Helicopter operations
close to the border have proved to be a potentially dangerous undertaking. Despite the variety of manoeuvres employed by helicopter pilots the
terrorist still regards the helicopter shoot as a relatively easy and prestigious operation.'[16]

Buoyed by its recent successes, an emboldened PIRA now felt sufficiently confident to finally deploy their SA-7s.

Ever since it became clear that the Provisionals had received shoulder-launched SAMs from Gaddafi, the British had been nervously

awaiting their deployment in Northern Ireland. Garda intelligence reports indicated the Provos had test-fired an SA-7 in the Republic in 1988, but the IRA seemed reluctant to make use of the missiles across the border. The reason for this remains unclear, although at the time British military sources speculated that it may have been due to a lack of technical knowledge on how to operate them or that the Libyan SAMs were defective.

But on 19 July 1991 the long wait for PIRA to make their move came to an end. At 1420 hours two Wessex of 72 Squadron were on border patrol at the little County Fermanagh village of Kinawley when a projectile trailing smoke streaked close past the two choppers, before exploding in a field.

At first, there was some doubt as to whether or not it was a missile that had been fired at the aircraft. PIRA, no doubt wishing to conceal from the British the fact that they were now equipped with SAMs, added to the confusion when they released a statement insisting that they had used an RPG in the attack and claiming to have hit one of the helicopters, 'which,' the statement went on, 'was forced to withdraw during the attack' – something denied by the British Army.[17] Confirmation that an SA-7 had in fact been used only came seven weeks later when the tailfin of the missile was found in a field near the scene of the attack.

Whether the operator had failed to achieve a 'lock' before firing, the SAM malfunctioned, or the seeker head of the missile was defeated by the AN/ALQ-144 jammer, fitted to every helicopter stationed in Northern Ireland in 1988, remains a mystery. However, the SA-7 had a reputation for unreliability and was highly vulnerable to anti-missile countermeasures, performing poorly in the Soviet-Afghan War of the 1980s.[18]

Despite the failure of the attack, this first launch of a surface-to-air missile in Northern Ireland was a source of considerable anxiety to the security forces and sparked an intensive hunt for the SA-7s south of the border. 'The security forces in Northern Ireland are increasingly concerned that the Provos have become more expert in their use,' a Garda source said at the time, 'and so they have asked us to make an all-out effort to find the missiles.'[19] But the SA-7s remained frustratingly elusive, only one being recovered – in an underground concrete bunker near Athboy in

County Meath – by the time of PIRA's 1994 ceasefire. Fortunately, there were no further recorded SAM attacks before the end of the 'Troubles', either because the missiles were faulty or PIRA realized that the SA-7 was unlikely to penetrate the British helicopters' anti-missile defences.

For their next major attack, PIRA reverted to more dependable weaponry. On 16 March 1992 an ASU from the South Fermanagh brigade launched a sustained machine-gun attack on a pair of helicopters flying close to the border between Fermanagh and Monaghan, the Army confirming that 'two Lynx helicopters belonging to 655 Squadron were conducting a routine tasking in the Roslea area when they came under fire.'[20] According to PIRA's statement, 'Three machine guns and two rifles were used in the attack, in which more than 1,000 rounds were fired.' Although the statement also claimed that at least one of the helicopters was damaged, an inspection of the aircraft after landing back at base found that neither Lynx had been hit.

In a sign that the Provisionals' grip on their republican strongholds was beginning to weaken, such attacks were by now attracting increasingly outspoken criticism from within the local communities. After this helicopter shoot, one local lashed out: 'They gave no thought to the horrific consequences of what might have happened had the two machines gone out of control and crashed ... the thought of a helicopter hurtling down on to a house, a group of houses, a shop or a school does not bear contemplation.'[21]

Besides major pre-planned ambushes such as those described above, opportunity shootings at helicopters also took place, usually carried out by gunmen fleeing the scene of another attack. One such incident occurred on 12 August 1992 in Strabane, County Tyrone. At 1300 hours a PIRA gang which had taken over a house in the town, holding the family hostage, carried out a sniper attack on a passing foot patrol of the 2nd Bn Royal Green Jackets. Fortunately, they missed their target, the patrol commander. The gunmen then fled in a stolen Ford Sierra. As it sped towards a VCP, the soldiers manning the checkpoint opened fire, injuring one of the gunmen and badly damaging the Sierra. An RAF helicopter then joined the chase, 'whose pilot,' a court statement later revealed, 'brought the machine down to a height of 100 feet to obtain a better view'. The three gunmen, armed with AKM assault rifles, abandoned the shot-up Sierra in the Ballycolman industrial estate. 'At least one of these men fired a rifle at the helicopter, but did not register any hits'.[22] The gunmen fled into a nearby housing estate, pursued by the helicopter, now flying at a safer altitude of 1,500 feet, which was sealed off by the RUC. One injured volunteer was found hiding in one of the houses during the subsequent search.

Sixteen months later, in the early hours of 12 December 1993, RUC Constables William Beacom and Ernest Smyth were carrying out a mobile patrol in Fivemiletown, County Tyrone, when they were ambushed at a road junction by PIRA gunmen, who riddled their unmarked Renault with twenty shots, killing both men. An hour later, a Lynx involved in the follow-up search for the killers came under automatic rifle fire a few miles from the scene of the shooting. Again, the helicopter wasn't hit, but this time the gunmen escaped.

In the face of the escalating threat posed by the Gaddafi-armed PIRA, the British began to respond with a more aggressive use of airpower in the border areas, and would deliver some important blows to the terrorists during this most critical phase of the conflict in South Armagh.

Chapter Eight

Striking Back

On 20 February 1990 the RAF's Support Helicopter Force enjoyed one of its greatest successes against the South Armagh brigade, in an incident which, a 72 Squadron report recorded, 'was particularly noteworthy because in 20 years of SH operations in NI, helicopters were able for the first time to physically prevent a major terrorist action'.

Just nine days earlier Gazelle ZB687 had been brought down by ground fire in County Tyrone (see Chapter Seven) and aircrews were on high alert for another helicopter attack. On the afternoon of the 20th, having just dropped off a patrol from the 2nd Bn Light Infantry near Newtownhamilton, the pilot of a Wessex made out three figures wearing balaclavas, who were setting up several General Purpose Machine Guns in a clearing of a wooded area, apparently with the intention of carrying out a helicopter shoot. Before the gunmen could open fire, the Wessex swept in towards them, prompting the volunteers to abandon the attack and flee. 'Together with a second Wessex it followed the men, who drove off in 2 waiting vehicles with a number of other terrorists,' explained the 72 Squadron report.[1]

What followed was one of the longest helicopter chases of the 'Troubles', during which the fleeing PIRA gang hijacked several other cars, switching getaway vehicles no fewer than eight times in a desperate attempt to shake off their airborne pursuers. 'At one point,' revealed the ORB, 'automatic weapons were aimed at the lead aircraft but no shots fired.'[2] The Wessex pilots, however, were not deterred by the threat of PIRA fire and maintained the pursuit.

During the chase the gang threw their machine guns, ammunition and other incriminating evidence, including CB radios which they had been using to co-ordinate the planned helicopter shoot with their 'dickers', from the speeding cars. 'We couldn't shoot them if they were unarmed and they knew that,' explained one of the Light Infantry troops. 'And that's why they chucked their weapons out of the windows.'[3]

The chase, which stretched over seven miles, finally came to an end near Silverbridge when troops on the ground, guided in by the helicopters, captured three suspects as they tried to escape on foot after abandoning one of their getaway cars. But after being handed over to RUC officers a republican mob some forty-strong quickly gathered and began attacking the police, allowing the three to escape in the ensuing chaos.

Despite this, the security forces considered the afternoon's events a major success and the Wessex crews' actions came in for high praise. 'Congratulations have been received from the S of S [Secretary of State], HQNI, CINC [Commander in Chief] and AOC [Air Officer Commanding],' recorded 72's CO.[4] 'The alertness of the pilot,' added an RUC spokesman, 'undoubtedly prevented a major terrorist operation.'[5]

That a helicopter ambush had indeed been the gang's intention was later confirmed when follow-up searches of local properties uncovered what was described as a 'major PIRA Int [Intelligence] Cell'. Among other items recovered were videotapes PIRA had taken of helicopter movements in the area, the discovery of which, the 72 Squadron ORB remarked, 'will no doubt be a major setback for the PIRA'.[6] The tapes offered the security forces a valuable insight into the South Armagh brigade's anti-helicopter strategy. 'The IRA were getting more sophisticated,' said one of the Light Infantry troops. 'They were videoing every helicopter that flew over the area.'[7]

The major follow-up operation launched by the security forces also led to the arrest of four more suspects, while the haul of captured weaponry included two GPMGs, two AKMs and a Heckler & Koch G3 assault rifle, along with a quantity of ammunition, most of which originated from the Libyan shipments. The Squadron CO also praised the Wessex crews for showing 'great restraint in not opening fire during a prolonged and fast moving chase'.

However, while one of the South Armagh brigade's largest attempted helicopter ambushes, involving, the Army estimated, as many as twenty volunteers, had been successfully foiled and important intelligence gathered, 'the incident was worrying,' admitted an RAF officer, 'because of the scale of the terrorist operation … and the apparent ease with which men and weapons could be moved around the TAOR.'[8] Clearly, PIRA's stranglehold on South Armagh remained as firm as ever.

'the threat of machine gun attack against helicopters is real'

The threat presented to British control of the air by PIRA with its arsenal of heavy weapons supplied by Gaddafi prompted Army commanders to revisit the contentious issue of arming helicopters for self-defence.

In June 1989 Secretary of State for Northern Ireland Tom King admitted that the danger posed to military aircraft was escalating. '[T]he threat of machine gun attack against helicopters is real,' he told the Commons, adding that, 'a number of steps were taken some time ago to give all possible protection to helicopters in the important work that they do.'[9] Besides adding a co-pilot, these measures included the fitting of Kevlar armour to the belly panels of helicopters to protect the cabin's occupants from 12.7mm rounds and having helicopters fly in pairs in the border areas to provide mutual support.

Yet it wasn't until December, following one of the largest and most intense firefights between British troops and PIRA in many years, that the go-ahead was finally given for the arming of helicopters in Northern Ireland. In what the Army described as 'a highly co-ordinated, sophisticated direct assault', on 13 December 1989 an eleven-man ASU armed with Dushkas, RPGs and even a flamethrower launched a major assault on an isolated PVCP at Derryard in County Fermanagh, with the aim of overrunning and destroying the fortified base.

After suffering two fatal casualties in the initial onslaught, the handful of King's Own Scottish Borderers manning the PVCP, though outmanned and heavily outgunned, successfully held off the attackers until relieved by a four-man KOSB patrol led by Lance Corporal Ian Harvey (later awarded the Distinguished Conduct Medal for his actions, as was one of the base's defending soldiers, Corporal Robert Duncan), who were supported by a Wessex. The arrival of Lance Corporal Harvey's patrol forced the raiders to withdraw after a fierce exchange of fire, some of which was directed at the Wessex, whose pilot had to take evasive action. As the Wessex was unarmed, the crew were unable to retaliate against the gunmen, all of whom escaped. The Derryard attack, revealed the 72 Squadron ORB, 'led to the Bessbrook aircraft being fitted with GPMGs as a matter of routine'.[10] The arming of helicopters in Northern Ireland, along with other defensive measures to counter the growing PIRA threat, went by the codename Operation ATTAINMENT.[11]

However, highly restrictive rules of engagement imposed upon the door gunners now being carried on most helicopters in the border areas reduced the effectiveness of this new defensive measure. This was acknowledged by Army commanders in April 1991, who observed that, 'Although door guns have been fitted to Lynx for over a year there are severe limitations preventing their use'. Another limitation was the ineffective gun mount and sight initially fitted to the helicopters, a problem cited in the report into the downing of Lynx ZE380 on 13 February 1991. 'This incident,' reported Brigadier Tait, Commander of Aviation for UK Land Forces, 'highlights the urgency of the requirement for a really effective system.'[12]

Partly due to these problems, it wasn't until 1993 that Lynx door gunners finally got the opportunity to engage PIRA gunmen. Late on the afternoon of 8 January, a border patrol base at Mullan Bridge near Kinawley in Fermanagh, close to where the SA-7 missile had been launched at the two Wessex in the summer of 1991, came under mortar attack. Of the two mortars fired, one failed to explode while the second caused only minor damage to the base and no casualties. The attackers then opened fire at the base from positions just across the border.

Alerted by the mortar explosion, two Lynx quickly arrived at the scene with reinforcements. 'Shortly after firing at the PB [Patrol Base] the terrorists fired upon the two helicopters which were carrying the ARF to the area,' revealed the Army incident report.

Being in the Irish Republic, the gunmen probably considered themselves relatively safe from retaliatory action. But after the Lynx pilots successfully evaded PIRA's bullets, 'the door gunners began to lay down fire at a farm complex in the ROI [Republic Of Ireland],'[13] where the hostile fire was believed to be coming from, the report explained. The gunmen, estimated by the Lynx crews to number eight in all, were then observed by the crews fleeing in a yellow van before transferring to a truck and escaping.

Neither helicopter was damaged in the exchange, during which the door gunners fired a total of 200 rounds from their GPMGs. While no hits were claimed by either of the Lynx crews, one of the pilots is believed to have been awarded the first, and indeed only, Distinguished Flying Medal of Operation BANNER, 'in recognition of gallantry in Northern Ireland', the last such award before the DFM was discontinued in an overhaul of the British military honours system later that year.

The Battle of Newry Road

Nine months later a much larger gun battle took place between helicopter crews and PIRA, this time in the heart of South Armagh, in what PIRA itself described as 'the most intense ever to take place in the area'.[14]

It began shortly after 1400 hours on 23 September 1993. An hour earlier a force later estimated to number around thirty volunteers had quietly taken up firing positions around the Crossmaglen base. Heavily armed with Dushkas, GPMGs, RPG-7s and AK-47s, they were split into five groups, three of which were manning mobile gun platforms – two flatbed lorries and a Toyota pick-up – while another was positioned in a nearby wooded area. Their target was a Puma, which arrived at the base that afternoon on a re-supply flight, escorted by two armed Lynx, referred to as Lynx 1 and 2, the latter commanded by Staff Sergeant Shaun Wyatt of 655 Squadron. A former soldier in the Royal Artillery, Wyatt served in the Falklands War and undertook pilot training in 1991, earning that year's best student award.

As the Puma was just about to take off, the PIRA teams opened fire. In an interview years later, Wyatt recalled: 'I heard a tap, tap, tap, tap, tap: the thought ran through my head that surely this was not the sound of a gun.' As it became clear that they were indeed under fire, Wyatt radioed a contact report while his co-pilot quickly gained height. But he soon realized that the large Puma was the gunmen's intended target. 'I told the Puma to stay on the ground but it lifted off anyway and was hit by a round before climbing away above us,' Wyatt revealed.[15] The single 12.7mm round that struck the Puma caused no injuries.

The Lynx then came in low to identify the firing positions of the PIRA attackers, whereupon, Wyatt explained, 'we were again engaged by a further [firing] point, with a GPMG mounted on the back of a 4 x 4'. Evading the incoming stream of fire, they then gained altitude, and were joined by two more Lynx helicopters. Wyatt continued:

> We were now trying to find the terrorists and our door gunner reported that he could see two lorries travelling east out of Crossmaglen, and they looked like they had weapons on the back. I then took control of our aircraft and put it into a dive to get back to low level so we were below the threat band.[16]

Wyatt chased the two lorries, which were joined by a red car carrying several more volunteers, along the Newry Road and positioned his helicopter to block their escape route, with his door gunner facing the oncoming vehicles. 'When they were 500 or 600 metres away, I told the door gunner to open fire,' said Wyatt. Unfortunately, the GPMG jammed after firing just two rounds. 'We were gutted,' he admitted.

But the battle was only just beginning. The convoy of three PIRA vehicles headed towards their pre-arranged dispersal points, with the determined Wyatt in close pursuit, followed by two more Lynx. The gunmen on the fleeing lorries returned fire as the Lynx chased them through the narrow lanes of South Armagh, but, revealed Wyatt, whenever he managed to get his helicopter into a firing position 'our gun kept on jamming'.[17]

'I accelerated to get ahead of them,' he continued. Once he had done so, the pilot again used his Lynx to block the road the getaway vehicles were speeding along and ordered his door gunner to open fire – only for their 'Gimpy' to jam yet again after just a single brief burst.

One of the most successful two-seater fighters of the First World War, the Bristol F2B was the main type operated by the RAF in Ireland during the Anglo-Irish War.

An Auster AOP.6 of 13 Flight, 651 Squadron. Five of these reliable spotter planes were sent to Northern Ireland during the IRA's 'Border Campaign' of 1956-62. (© The International Auster Club)

A Westland Sioux AH1 on patrol over Londonderry in August 1972, shortly after Operation CARCAN. (© Eamon Melaugh)

To offer greater protection to crews as the violence in Northern Ireland intensified, in the early 1970s the Army tested machine-gun-armed Sioux and Scout helicopters. However, it would be many years before helicopters in the province were routinely armed.
(Courtesy of www.flyingmarines.com)

A typically busy scene at Bessbrook Mill, centre of helicopter operations in South Armagh, in the early 1990s. (© Museum of Army Flying)

The well-liked de Havilland Canada Beaver AL1 provided sterling service in the reconnaissance role in Northern Ireland from 1973 until 1989. (© BAE SYSTEMS)

The Westland/Aérospatiale SA 341 Gazelle proved to be an excellent surveillance platform. This Gazelle of the Royal Marines' Commando Brigade Air Squadron is equipped with the powerful 'Nitesun' searchlight. (courtesy of www.flyingmarines.com)

IRA volunteers pose for the camera with Browning M2 heavy machine guns, used in several helicopter ambushes in the 1980s. (© Victor Patterson)

Wessex XR506 of 72 Squadron. This aircraft survived two major IRA attacks in July 1982 and May 1983. (Aviation Photo Company)

Test-firing of an FIM-92 Stinger in a NATO exercise. During the 1980s the IRA became obsessed with obtaining these formidable SAMs. (© US Department of Defense)

The DShK 'Dushka'. The Provisionals received a consignment of these Russian heavy machine guns from Libya in the mid-1980s, greatly enhancing their anti-aircraft capability. (iStock)

Potent propaganda. A republican mural in west Belfast depicting the shooting down of a Lynx helicopter in South Armagh in 1988. (© Tony Crowley)

A Westland Lynx AH7 with a door gunner manning a GPMG comes in to land in a South Armagh field. By 1990 the threat of ground fire in the border areas led to the routine arming of helicopters in Northern Ireland. (© Museum of Army Flying)

A view of a 'Romeo' watchtower in South Armagh from the position of a Lynx door gunner. (Courtesy of Airborne Assault Archives, Duxford)

Arriving in Northern Ireland in 1989, the Britten-Norman Islander AL1 replaced the venerable de Havilland Canada Beaver as the Army Air Corps' fixed-wing 'eye in the sky'. (© David Townsend)

End of a mission. An RAF Chinook of 7 Squadron airlifting a section of a 'Romeo' watchtower in South Armagh in October 2001 as part of the Army's demilitarization programme in the final years of Operation BANNER. (© Donald MacLeod)

It wasn't just the Lynx crew who were suffering weapon malfunctions that day. PIRA was also experiencing jamming problems during the initial exchanges, as the South Armagh brigade admitted in their statement issued after the incident: 'units encountered some mechanical difficulties when a number of other heavy weapons jammed, thus seriously reducing the planned weight of IRA firepower.'[18]

After Wyatt's door gunner cleared his stoppage they resumed the chase. 'I then tried to get directly above the convoy so we could shoot down on them, but they couldn't fire on us,' Wyatt explained. The PIRA convoy split up, the crew losing track of the red car while one of the lorries veered off towards a farm and disappeared into a barn. Wyatt's crew then turned their attention to the second lorry. Frustratingly, however, just as the door gunner was about to open up on it one of the other pursuing Lynx 'flew through our line of fire', forcing them to break off the attack.[19]

The second lorry was then abandoned in the centre of a village and the Lynx crew watched as the PIRA gun team transferred their weapons to a white Ford Transit, which they were unable to fire on due to the proximity of innocent civilians, and resumed the pursuit as the van headed south towards the border.

Meanwhile, another Lynx had returned to Crossmaglen to collect a six-man ARF of the 1st Bn Duke of Edinburgh's Royal Regiment and landed the troops in a field along the van's escape route. The soldiers engaged the van, forcing it to a halt. Three masked volunteers leapt out, leaving behind their weapons, and ran into a nearby bungalow from which they emerged seconds later and sped off in a hijacked car.

Having been stymied by weapon jams, another helicopter crossing their line of fire and the presence of civilians, the crew of Wyatt's Lynx were now thwarted by the Yellow Card rules of engagement. 'I followed the car but didn't open fire because I couldn't say, hand on heart, that the three men who ran out of the bungalow were definitely the men who had run into it moments earlier,' he explained.

The suspect car escaped across the border, while Wyatt returned to the barn where the other flatbed gun lorry had taken refuge from the British helicopters. 'But,' he revealed, 'everyone had gone by the time we arrived.'[20]

This epic running gun battle, which stretched over twelve miles and lasted some thirty minutes, and during which over 200 rounds were fired by the Lynx gunners, was said to have been the largest of its kind in South Armagh during the 'Troubles'. One witness, Crossmaglen publican Paddy Short, remarked afterwards: 'We have had gun battles here before but this must have been one of the longest. Both sides were having a right go at each other.'

Clearly rattled by the strength of the opposition they encountered from the armed helicopters, the South Armagh brigade released a statement containing a highly inaccurate version of the events. Claiming that 'the British fired indiscriminately from the helicopter onto houses, farms and any vehicle moving around the scene of the shooting', the statement even insisted that the Lynx helicopters had fired rockets during the chase,[21] despite the fact that no helicopter based in Northern Ireland was armed with such weapons.

Although the gunmen managed to slip away, in a massive follow-up operation by the security forces, which saw hundreds of troops and police descend on the area, two arrests were made and a Dushka, an assault rifle and two GPMGs, along with hundreds of rounds of ammunition, captured. Praising the actions of the helicopter crews, RUC Assistant Chief Constable William Stewart said: 'Everyone owes a great debt of gratitude to these men.'

Shortly afterwards Staff Sergeant Wyatt was promoted to Warrant Officer Class 2 and awarded the Distinguished Flying Cross for his role in what became known as 'The Battle of Newry Road', which he received from the Queen at an investiture at Buckingham Palace in July 1994.

Improving Co-operation

PIRA was also coming under increasing pressure due to enhanced cross-border security co-operation between the Irish and British authorities. As we have seen, perceived lack of support from Dublin in countering terrorist activity along the border had long been a source of friction between the two governments. But following the signing of the Anglo-Irish Agreement in November 1985, which gave Dublin an advisory role in the running of Northern Ireland's affairs in exchange for enhanced efforts against the terrorists, security co-operation steadily improved.

Among the measures introduced was new legislation passed by the Dáil in 1987 making it easier to extradite terrorist suspects from the Republic to the UK, while the Garda also increased its presence along the border. This paid off on 23 October 1989, when a six-man PIRA ASU was discovered by a patrol of Gardaí at Corlea near the border between Counties Donegal and Fermanagh whilst setting up a Dushka to attack a British helicopter. Although the volunteers managed to escape into a wooded area, they were forced to leave behind the heavy machine gun, along with several spare barrels.

In the wake of the downing of the Lynx on 23 June 1988, finding PIRA's small stockpile of powerful DShK HMGs was regarded as a priority by both the British and Irish security forces, and to this end the Garda launched a series of major search operations throughout the Republic.

Their first success came in July 1988 when they found a PIRA arms dump at Borris-in-Ossory in County Laois containing a single Dushka, with another being recovered two months later in County Carlow. Two more were captured, along with several RPGs, during the Garda's Operation SILO in 1992, which uncovered a network of seventeen underground arms storage bunkers in the Munster area, and a further pair in another concrete bunker was discovered in County Meath in July 1994.

The Provisionals were also losing some of their prized Dushkas in attacks on the security forces in Northern Ireland that went wrong. In February 1992 one of the machine guns fell into the hands of the British when an SAS team ambushed and killed four PIRA volunteers after they attacked an RUC station with a DShK machine gun mounted on a flatbed lorry in Coalisland, County Tyrone.

While the security forces north and south of the border were steadily depleting PIRA's arsenal of heavy weapons, the British were stepping up aerial surveillance of the terrorists in South Armagh. From the mid-1970s a number of Scouts in Northern Ireland were equipped with a video-surveillance system known as 'Heli-Tele', but by the late 1980s this had been superseded by the much more advanced 'Chancellor' system, which consisted of a digital video camera mounted in a spherical pod carried externally on a Lynx, which relayed images to bases in real-time via data link.

Meanwhile, in June 1989, the last of the Army's long-serving de Havilland Canada Beavers were finally retired from service. Their replacement in Northern Ireland as the AAC's fixed-wing eye in the sky was the Britten-Norman Islander AL1, five of which formed 1 Flight the first arriving at RAF Aldergrove on 10 March 1989.

First taking to the air in 1965, the twin-engined Islander was a more capable surveillance platform than the well-liked but elderly Beaver. Not only was it faster, quieter and with greater endurance (being able to stay in the air for up to four hours), it could also carry twice as many passengers and was kitted out with more advanced surveillance equipment.

Like the Beaver, its primary role was photographic reconnaissance, for which it was fitted with several powerful Zeiss cameras, mounted in the belly of the aircraft. Although many aspects of the Islanders' role in Northern Ireland remain classified, 1 Flight's aircraft are also believed to have carried out an electronic intelligence-gathering function, though this has never been confirmed. As with the helicopter fleet, since 1994 the Aldergrove-based Islanders were also fitted with the AN/ALQ-144 Infra-Red jammer to counter the threat from MANPADS.

The 'Sneaky Beaky Flight'

Even more secretive than 1 Flight and its Islanders was a small flight of Gazelles, said to have been known informally as the 'Bat Flight' (and even more informally as the 'Sneaky Beaky Flight'), with hand-picked pilots, whose job was to support the operations of 14 Intelligence Company. Known as 'The Det' (short for Detachment), 14 Intelligence Company was the British Army's elite covert surveillance unit in Northern Ireland and served in the province from 1974, often working in conjunction with the SAS.

The operations of the Flight have been, and remain, cloaked in secrecy and little information about the unit's involvement in Operation

BANNER has emerged. One Army Air Corps pilot who served with the Flight in the late 1980s said: 'I did two years on the "Sneaky Beaky Flight". That was a fantastic tour. Intelligence-gathering ... you name it, we did it. We weren't governed by the normal flying restrictions.'[22]

The Gazelles carried TI (Thermal Imaging) equipment and other sensors to allow 14 Intelligence Company operatives to track terrorist suspects. One member of 'The Det' revealed that the helicopters could loiter at 8,000 feet (at which height they would be virtually inaudible to those on the ground) and with their powerful sights could observe the door of a house below.[23] 'The Gazelle was the ideal platform for this role,' confirmed AAC pilot Ed Macy, who served with 655 Squadron in South Armagh in the 1990s. 'Thanks to its powerful high resolution, thermal-imaging camera system, we could stare down the throats of any-one down there.' [24]

PIRA grew increasingly wary of surveillance helicopters. Volunteer Gerry Bradley estimated that by the early 1990s as much as 80 per cent of their planned attacks had to be abandoned due to the presence of surveil-lance aircraft. 'The chopper destroyed us,' he admitted. 'If the chopper was up, you weren't allowed to move out of a house: [PIRA] army orders. Ops were cancelled regularly because of [helicopters] ... if the chopper spots one major player in the wrong place, that's it, an op is ruined.'[25]

Besides airborne surveillance and intelligence-gathering, in the early 1990s the SAS devised another role for helicopters. As attacks on military aircraft operating in South Armagh mounted, they came up with a high-risk plan to snare one of PIRA's anti-aircraft ambush teams by using AAC Lynx, armed with concealed .50 Browning M2 heavy machine guns, as bait.

Staff Sergeant Gaz Hunter, who served as the SAS's Operations Officer in South Armagh, revealed that after receiving intelligence indi-cating that the South Armagh brigade were planning a helicopter attack using Dushkas an SAS team flew around the danger area in helicopters equipped with .50 Brownings behind sandbags in the cabin, hoping to lure out the PIRA ambush team and mount a counter-attack.[26]

Black Watch soldier Corporal Tam Henderson remembered another similar operation his patrol was involved in during the regiment's two-year resident tour in South Armagh in the early 1990s. On this occasion it was suspected that PIRA were planning an SA-7 missile attack. Corporal Henderson and his men were to be flown into the area where the attack was thought likely to take place, while a second armed helicopter would stand off close by, ready to respond if PIRA put in an appearance.

Although no attack materialized on either occasion, thanks to the alertness of one Wessex crew a PIRA team was captured whilst preparing to mount a helicopter ambush around this time and in the process turned an embarrassing incident for the British Army into a notable success against the East Tyrone brigade.

The chain of events leading to this success began on 17 May 1992 when a 'brick' of the 1st Bn King's Own Scottish Borderers became involved in an ugly confrontation with a hostile republican crowd in Coalisland, County Tyrone. During the fracas the patrol's GPMG was seized by a member of the crowd and passed on to a local unit of PIRA's East Tyrone brigade. A major security operation was immediately launched in the area to recover the weapon, with intelligence suggesting that PIRA planned to use it to attack a high profile security forces' target, in order to maximize the Army's discomfort over the embarrassing loss of the machine gun. The target the East Tyrone brigade settled on was a helicopter.

Eleven days later a three-man ASU set up a firing point by a farmhouse near the village of Cappagh in County Tyrone, mounting the stolen GPMG on an oil drum, which was to be used as a firing platform. At around 1700 hours the PIRA volunteers prepared to attack a Wessex as it was landing a joint RUC/Army patrol in the area when the crew 'noticed three men acting suspiciously in a field close to their drop off'.[27] Before they had a chance to open fire a foot patrol from the 3rd Bn Parachute Regiment, directed to their positions by the Wessex crew, moved in, forcing the gunmen to abandon their weapons and flee at high speed in a hijacked Ford Escort, closely pursued by the Wessex. 'The helicopter followed the car and saw one of the occupants running from it,' confirmed a police source.[28] He was quickly captured by troops set down by the Wessex, while the other members of the gang abandoned the Escort after setting it on fire in an attempt to destroy evidence, and fled on foot. Several more suspects were arrested in follow-up operations.

Back at the farmhouse, meanwhile, police and soldiers recovered the stolen machine gun, along with a second GPMG, an AKM assault rifle and 500 rounds of ammunition. One of the captured suspects was later convicted of conspiring to shoot down a military aircraft and sentenced to seventeen years.[29]

Right up to PIRA's August 1994 ceasefire helicopters continued to play an important role in the capture of terrorist suspects. On 12 August 1994, in one of the South Armagh brigade's last major attacks before the ceasefire came into effect, three mortars were fired at the Army watchtower at Glasdrumman, without inflicting any casualties. A nearby helicopter was called in, which tracked the two men suspected of carrying out the attack to a house in the village of Creggan, near Crossmaglen, where both were captured. For the Army this was a particularly sweet success, as one of the arrested men was also suspected of involvement in the Warrenpoint bombing fifteen years earlier.

But the months leading up to the historic ceasefire, which finally brought hope of an end to the violence after decades of bloodshed, would also prove to be some of the most dangerous for helicopter crews during the 'Troubles', as the South Armagh brigade unleashed a devastating new weapon.

Chapter Nine

Home-Made Solutions

On the surface, there was absolutely nothing unusual about Richard Clark Johnson. The quiet 40-year-old electrical engineer from Connecticut led what appeared to be an existence of banal normality. Unmarried and with few friends, he seemed to have little life outside his work.

But this unassuming man had for years been leading a double life as the Provisional IRA's top electronics expert in North America, whose secret work for the Provos had helped transform the organization into one of the world's most technologically sophisticated terrorist groups. In the early 1980s he helped PIRA develop a new type of radio control bomb detonator, which was first used in South Armagh in 1983.

On 15 December 1988 PIRA contacted Johnson again with a new project for which they needed his technical know-how. Calling from San Francisco, his contact, later identified as Martin Peter Quigley, a PIRA suspect from Dundalk who was studying computing at Pennsylvania's Lehigh University, explained the situation over the phone to Johnson: 'We're experiencing a slight technical problem .... You kinda helped us out of these situations before and we're looking to you once again.'[1] After Johnson assured Quigley he was willing to assist, the Irishman went on to outline the nature of the project. 'We're developing a new system, OK? It's kind of a new surface SAM system. And it's to counteract low-flying helicopters'.[2]

PIRA were developing their very own anti-aircraft surface-to-air missile launcher, with a maximum range of around 3,000 feet, intended for use in Northern Ireland against British helicopters. They needed Johnson's help to design and build a guidance system and proximity fuse for the weapon, which would explode the missile's warhead within a few feet of the target aircraft. After further discussing the technical details of the project, an enthusiastic Johnson assured Quigley that he would immediately begin work on the system. Unknown to either man, however, their conversation was being recorded by the FBI, who had bugged the payphone in Nashua, New Hampshire, from which Johnson had received Quigley's call.

Richard Clark Johnson had first come to the FBI's attention five years earlier, after the RUC traced the components of a sophisticated frequency-hopping radio-control detonator, used in a PIRA bomb that exploded in Bessbrook on 3 September 1983, to the US. The investigation was then taken up by the FBI, with the trail eventually leading to Johnson, who had bought the electrical components and at the time was based in California, where he worked for the Northrop Corporation, one of America's biggest defence companies.

Johnson's interest in electronics began at a young age. 'He had a scientific mind and was always interested in radios, telescopes and things like that,' said his mother Anne.[3] After gaining a Master's degree in electrical engineering from California's Berkeley University in 1972, he secured jobs with major US defence contractors including Hughes Aircraft and Northrop, working on classified projects for the US military.

An Irish-American, whose grandparents were originally from Kerry and Cork, it's believed Johnson was recruited by PIRA during a visit to Ireland in 1976 and, according to the FBI, from 1978 'was engaged in research and development of explosives for export to the Republic of Ireland and use by the Provisional Irish Republican Army in its attacks against British civilian and military targets'.

Federal agents twice questioned Johnson in the mid-1980s about components used in at least two bombings in South Armagh which they believed he had sent to PIRA, but didn't have sufficient evidence to charge him. Nevertheless, from July 1988 they mounted long-term surveillance of Johnson, who was by now living in the New Hampshire town of Nashua and working on ECM projects for the Mitre Corporation, work for which he held a high-level security clearance.

After four months of surveillance, with nothing to show for their efforts, the FBI were preparing to wind down their investigation when they suddenly caught a break. In November 1988 Johnson got a call from a woman identifying herself as 'Chris'. This turned out to be Christina Reid, a 24-year-old electronics student from San Francisco, who acted as a go-between for Johnson and PIRA, putting the engineer in touch with Quigley so that he could help them out with the 'technical problem' they were experiencing with their latest weapon, a surface-to-air missile launcher.

Throughout the 'Troubles' the Provisionals devoted considerable resources to building their own weapons through their 'Engineering Department', for reasons both of prestige and to avoid becoming overly dependent on insecure foreign sources of arms supply. Among these weapons were hand grenades, improvised RPGs known as PRIGs (Projected Recoilless Improvised Grenades) and a wide range of mortars.

But designing and building a guided SAM system was by far PIRA's most ambitious undertaking, and illustrates the lengths to which the organization was prepared to go in its bid to make the skies of South Armagh and the border regions too dangerous for British helicopters.

Working primarily from a workshop in the basement of his parents' house in Harwich, Massachusetts, Johnson laboured over the proximity fuses and radar-guidance system for the next six months, whilst periodically meeting up with Quigley, whose job was to develop the missiles, to discuss the project. Both men were completely ignorant of the fact that all their conversations were being listened in to by the FBI, who had bugged both Johnson's and his parents' homes. Besides his work on the SAM launcher, Johnson was also advising Quigley on how to overcome the ECM equipment British soldiers now routinely carried whilst patrolling in South Armagh, which jammed radio-control signals used to detonate bombs and was responsible for the increasing number of failed PIRA attacks on foot patrols.

But the FBI's surveillance operation was blown on 12 July 1989 when Johnson disturbed two agents as they were fixing a listening device in his car, which was parked outside his workplace. By then, however, the FBI had accumulated enough evidence to arrest Johnson, Quigley and

Reid, along with a fourth conspirator, Gerald Hoy, and charge them with 'conspiracy to injure and destroy the property of a foreign government'. At Johnson's basement workshop investigators found bomb detonation devices, while a search of Quigley's apartment in Pennsylvania uncovered a near-complete prototype of the anti-aircraft weapon, along with a videotape of one of the suspects test-firing a missile. A fifth suspect, Eamon McGuire (the man alleged by the CIA to have been PIRA's 'chief technical officer'), escaped and fled to Nigeria but was later captured and extradited to the US.

At a press conference held after the arrests, FBI special agent James Ahearn said that, 'It appears quite clear that they were doing a two-fold operation: building a radar deliverance system, and developing rocket technology aimed at something – and the something appears at the very least to be British helicopters.'[4] FBI director William Sessions added that the arrest of Johnson and the seized equipment 'demonstrate the high level of technical sophistication being employed by terrorist organisations to further violence worldwide.'[5]

Their trial began in Boston in May 1990, prosecutor Richard Stearns declaring in his opening statement that 'shooting down helicopters has been a fixation of the IRA for almost two decades'. The court also heard how, in one bugged conversation, Quigley described to Johnson another idea he'd been toying with for destroying helicopters - floating balloons trailing Kevlar ropes, with grenades attached to the ends, into the path of a helicopter in the hope that the ropes would become entangled in the rotors and draw the grenades into the aircraft.[6] Although the plan sounded somewhat hare-brained, the former commander of the Northern Ireland Regiment AAC, Lieutenant Colonel Michael Webb, who was called to give evidence at the trial by the prosecution, insisted that such a weapon could present a serious threat. 'My opinion is it would cause catastrophic damage to the rotor system,' he testified. 'It would cause the helicopter to crash.'[7]

Throughout the trial the defence maintained that their clients were merely model rocket enthusiasts, with no terrorist connections. But the jury was unconvinced and the three were found guilty in June 1990 (the fourth defendant, Gerald Hoy, had already pleaded guilty). Quigley, Reid and Hoy received eight, three and two years respectively, while Johnson got the heaviest sentence at ten years. Special Agent Neil Gallagher, one of the investigators involved in the case, said that the successful FBI operation 'stopped [PIRA's] ability to shoot down low-flying British helicopters. It saved untold numbers of innocent lives.'[8]

Johnson's conviction put paid to PIRA's hopes of deploying its own SAM system. But the South Armagh brigade had another 'home-made' weapon in its armoury for attacking helicopters, one which, after much trial and error, would eventually bring them considerable success.

Mortars vs helicopters

Early in the conflict in Northern Ireland PIRA realized that the mortar would be an ideal stand-off weapon for attacking static targets, such as security forces bases. The advantages of such weapons were obvious: simple to operate and packing a big punch, mortars could be constructed using commercially available materials and fired a relatively safe distance from the target, greatly reducing the risks to the operator. The main disadvantage was that, being an area attack weapon, mortars were fairly inaccurate and presented a huge risk to any civilians in the vicinity of the target, though that did not appear to have overly concerned PIRA.

The South Armagh brigade in particular embraced the home-made mortar, and it was in South Armagh where most of PIRA's latest models were first deployed. By 1985 a British Army weapons intelligence report disclosed that the South Armagh IRA had amassed 'a considerable amount of mortar attack expertise'.[9] Eight years later an Army assessment of captured examples of PIRA's latest mortars found that they were 'extremely well made and may easily be mistaken for military models'.[10]

The Provisional IRA's first attack with such a weapon was carried out in May 1972, and they continued at a regular pace throughout the rest of the decade. These early mortars were quite crude and unreliable, and sometimes proved a greater danger to the operators than to British soldiers. For instance, on 16 August 1973 PIRA volunteers Patrick Quinn and Daniel McAnallen were loading a bomb into a Mk 3 mortar they were using to attack an RUC station at Pomeroy, County Tyrone, when the launch tube exploded, killing both men. In fact, in over seventy mortar attacks carried out between 1972 and 1978, the British Army suffered just a single fatal casualty – an ATO killed whilst defusing an unexploded mortar bomb in Lurgan, north Armagh, in December 1972.

PIRA's engineers were nothing if not persistent, however, and in 1979 they finally produced an effective model, one which was fairly reliable and could achieve a reasonable degree of accuracy. Designated the Mk 10 by British Army weapons analysts, it comprised up to ten launch tubes, which lobbed bombs a metre in length made from oxy-acetylene gas cylinders, each containing twenty kilograms of explosives, over a range of up to 200 metres. Most were triggered by command-wire or timer, thus minimizing the risk to the firer.

First used against the Army's base in Newtownhamilton on 19 March 1979, in which a soldier of the 3rd Bn The Queen's Regiment was killed, it was a Mk 10 mortar that was responsible for the single heaviest loss of life suffered by the RUC during the 'Troubles', when a mortar bomb killed nine officers in their station in Newry on 28 February 1985, and the attack on Downing Street on 7 February 1991.

The increasing threat posed by PIRA's mortars in the 1980s forced the Army to embark on a massive and costly programme to fortify its bases in an effort to make them more resistant to mortar bombs.

Besides Army bases and police stations, the South Armagh brigade realized that the Mk 10 mortar might also be an effective weapon for use against helicopters as they came in to the hover before landing at border bases, when they were at their most vulnerable.

The first such attack was carried out on 22 June 1983, six weeks after the heavy machine-gun attack on Wessex XR506 near Silverbridge (see Chapter Six). During the morning a dozen-strong ASU quietly took over the Lismore housing estate in Crossmaglen, going door-to-door and ordering residents whose homes were in the line of fire of the security forces base to leave, before blocking traffic on the Dundalk Road leading into the town. They then drove in a lorry carrying a Mk 10 and parked it 200 metres from the base. Around midday, as a Wessex carrying a USL came in to the hover above the base, the watching PIRA men triggered the mortars by command wire.

Spotting the volley of long, black projectiles arcing towards him, the startled pilot, a flying officer, swung his aircraft out of their path, the USL hitting the roof of a butcher's shop next door to the base in the process and causing its cargo of sandbags to spill out across the street. Ten mortars in all were fired, none of which hit the helicopter. Four failed to explode while the others landed around the perimeter fence of the base, damaging a guard tower and slightly wounding a soldier on sentry duty. The pilot flew his undamaged Wessex back to Bessbrook Mill.

The subsequent investigation found that the Wessex survived due to the mortar base plate having been misaligned by five to ten degrees; 'otherwise', the Squadron ORB admitted, 'the incident would have been a disaster, and a major propaganda success for the terrorists.' No. 72 Squadron's CO added defiantly that the near-miss brought 'no deterioration in morale nor our determination to carry out our task'.[11]

Almost two years to the day later, on the afternoon of 23 June 1985, a virtual carbon-copy attack took place when PIRA fired three mortars at another 72 Squadron Wessex flying into the same base. An NCO of the 1st Bn King's Own Scottish Borderers based in the area at the time later recalled:

> The Wessex loadmaster was hanging out, on a strap. He looked up and he said, 'They're mortaring'. He'd actually seen the mortars coming in and shouted to the pilot who sent the contact report straightaway. I think he probably sent that contact report before the first mortar hit the deck.[12]

Again, the Wessex wasn't hit. The commander of the KOSB company stationed at Crossmaglen heard what he described as 'three mega-f***ing explosions' as the mortar rounds landed inside the base perimeter, almost hitting an Army helicopter on the helipad. He took off in a Gazelle to locate the mortar vehicle, a van with a hole cut in the roof camouflaged with spray-painted cardboard through which the mortars had been fired, but by that time the attackers had fled the scene.

Having failed to take down helicopters in the air with mortars, the South Armagh brigade next tried to destroy them on the ground by attacking their main base, Bessbrook Mill. On 16 April 1987 PIRA fired thirteen mortar rounds at the base, four of which exploded inside the perimeter, hitting the HQ building and injuring two soldiers but failing to damage any of the aircraft sitting on their helipads. Two more bombs went off course and exploded in the village itself. 'The ground literally shook,' said one shaken Bessbrook resident.[13]

The guerrillas then moved on to a new design, the Mk 12. This was more akin to a rocket launcher than a mortar; rather than lobbing a bomb at a vertical angle, like a conventional mortar, it fired a sixty centimetre-long projectile, containing just over two kilograms of Semtex, horizontally. The Mk 12 made its first appearance in Northern Ireland in October 1989, three soldiers being injured when one was fired at the Crossmaglen base.

However, its heavy recoil, modest range and unreliable warhead, which frequently failed to detonate, were serious drawbacks, and it wasn't until 1 March 1991 that PIRA succeeded in killing security forces personnel with one. On that day an Army Land Rover stopped at traffic lights near Armagh City was hit by a Mk 12 concealed in the garden of a nearby house, killing one UDR soldier outright and fatally wounding another.

Five months later, on 2 August, a Puma of 33 Squadron was targeted with a Mk 12. Three missiles were fired simultaneously by radio control from a triple-tube launcher whilst troops disembarked from the helicopter at the Newtownhamilton security forces base. One of the missiles failed to detonate while the other two streaked past the Puma, exploding well beyond the target.

After almost a decade, the South Armagh brigade had yet to enjoy any success with their attempts to destroy helicopters with mortars. But even as more moderate elements within PIRA began exploring a possible political solution to the interminable conflict, in the early 1990s the organization's engineers were busy working on a new model of mortar that was to become their most devastating yet, one that would herald a much more dangerous phase of the conflict for aircrews operating in Bandit Country.

'A truly terrifying weapon'

On 5 December 1992 the RUC station at Ballygawley, County Tyrone, was rocked by a massive explosion, which injured several policemen. Though nobody had been killed, the police officers at Ballygawley had earned the dubious distinction of being the first to experience an attack by the newest and most destructive of PIRA's home-made mortars – the Mk 15.

Dubbed the 'barrack buster' by republicans and described as 'a truly terrifying weapon' by one ATO,[14] it was designed in response to the security forces' programme of fortifying their bases in the border areas during the 1980s, in the wake of the Newry disaster in February 1985. The barrack-buster had both range and a formidable payload, hurling a domestic gas cylinder a metre long by thirty-six centimetres wide, containing seventy-five kilograms of explosives, over a maximum distance of 275 metres. It became the Provos' standard mortar during the latter years of the 'Troubles', with around fifty attacks being carried out between December 1992 and the ceasefire of August 1994.

Seven months after making its operational debut at Ballygawley, the barrack buster was deployed for the first time by the South Armagh brigade in an anti-helicopter attack. The operation was timed to coincide with a one-day visit to the province by the Queen on 11 June 1993. At 1500 hours a single Mk 15 was launched at a Puma of 230 Squadron as it was taking off from the Crossmaglen base. 'The mortar was fired from a van disguised to resemble a local baker's delivery van which is frequently seen in the area,' explained the 230 Squadron ORB. 'Lynx 5 and 7 were providing mutual support at the time, but failed to notice anything suspicious.' Although the follow-up investigation found that the mortar had been carefully aimed at the HLS, the pilot managed to take off just before the giant barrack buster exploded on the helipad. This incident 'confirmed the intention of PIRA to obtain a "spectacular" with an attack on a helicopter.'[15]

The South Armagh brigade's persistence finally paid off on 19 March 1994. That night, a Lynx of 655 Squadron was due to arrive at the Crossmaglen base carrying an underslung load. 'The threat against helicopters during the day was extremely high at that time,' explained Sergeant Major 'D' of the 1st Bn Grenadier Guards, who was stationed in the base's operations room that day. 'For this reason administrative and re-supply flights were generally carried out in the dark, as this was deemed safer.'

Lynx 5, as it was designated, duly appeared over the base just before 2030 hours carrying its USL and a single passenger, RUC Constable Pete Skelly. As it hovered around 100 feet above the helipad, being directed in from the ground by Lance Corporal Wayne Cuckson of the Royal Logistic Corps, a power cut plunged the base and the entire town into darkness. Seconds later, recalled Sergeant Major 'D', there was 'a tremendous bang, the room shook and plaster and dust fell from the roof.'[16]

A Mk 15 mortar had struck the tail boom of the Lynx and brought it crashing down into the base, where it immediately burst into flames. 'The first thing the crew was aware of was a very loud bang and loss of directional stability,' an AAC pilot stationed in South Armagh explained to the press shortly after the attack. 'The aircraft has got to come to a hover at some stage over the base ... but we obviously minimize the length of time that we spend in the hover, particularly low level over that area.'[17]

When Sergeant Major 'D' rushed out of the operations room he was greeted by what he described as 'a scene of devastation'. He recalled that the stricken helicopter 'was sitting upright on its underslung load', its tail boom completely severed. He added that, 'the cockpit of the helo was completely engulfed in flames and it looked really bad for anyone still on board.'[18]

Remarkably, however, the three crewmen escaped with only minor injuries. But realizing Constable Skelly was still trapped inside the blazing wreckage, they and Lance Corporal Cuckson rushed back to the crash site to rescue the badly wounded Skelly, whose abdomen had been cut open by a shard of flying Perspex.

By this time the flames licking around the wreckage of the Lynx were causing ammunition from the door gunner's GPMG to 'cook off', serving as an additional hazard to the rescuers. Nevertheless, Lance Corporal Cuckson and the crew managed to drag the constable to safety, just moments before the helicopter's fuel tanks exploded.

With the burning wreckage blocking the helipad, the wounded Constable Skelly was taken to a nearby field in a Saxon armoured personnel carrier, where another helicopter arrived shortly afterwards to evacuate him to hospital. Despite his injuries, the officer went on to make a full recovery.

Lance Corporal Cuckson was awarded the Queen's Gallantry Medal, while the Lynx's door gunner was Mentioned in Despatches for helping in the rescue of the injured RUC constable. The crew's actions throughout the drama came in for high praise. 'The skill displayed by the crew of the helicopter undoubtedly avoided a major tragedy,' said an RUC spokesman. 'Although the aircraft was completely disabled, the pilot managed to bring it down within the base. Had it crash-landed in the town itself, many lives would have been put at risk.'[19]

When the Army located the mortar firing point, a tractor parked on waste ground around 150 metres from the base, investigators were able to piece together exactly how PIRA had carried out the attack. 'The method of firing the mortar at exactly the right time was ingenious,' conceded a member of the Army EOD team tasked to deal with the incident. It was discovered that PIRA had used a command collapsing circuit, which triggered the mortar after they cut the power supply to the village from an electricity sub-station, which was responsible for the black-out that struck Crossmaglen. PIRA were known to have used such a method to detonate a device only once before, on 29 June 1982, when they set off a bomb hidden in a house whilst an ATO defused a mortar abandoned nearby.

In their statement claiming responsibility, the South Armagh brigade insisted: 'The operation was well planned by our engineers and carefully executed to avoid civilian casualties.' Moderate nationalist politicians begged to differ. 'God knows how many people could have been killed. When you realize this mortar was lobbed over a number of houses, it brings home the enormity of the danger so many people faced,' said Seamus Mallon, SDLP MP for Newry and Armagh,[20] while a councillor for the Crossmaglen area, John Fee, went further, calling the attack 'an act of lunacy' and declaring that 'local people are absolutely sick of terrorists in this area.' Fee's outspoken condemnation earned him a severe beating at his home by two masked men a few days later. Though the Provos denied responsibility, Fee had no doubts as to who was behind the assault. 'The IRA, I believe, felt they had to create a high-profile way of telling people, "Keep your mouth shut,"' he told the press afterwards.[21]

And again …

By now, the Provisional IRA ceasefire that would pave the way for the Belfast Agreement was on the horizon. But even as PIRA's campaign elsewhere in Northern Ireland was dwindling in the face of the increasing pressure being brought to bear on the organization by the security forces, the South Armagh brigade remained determined to carry out further 'spectaculars', so that the Provisionals' political representatives could enter talks with the British government from a position of strength.

As such, less than four months after the destruction of the Lynx, on 12 July – traditionally a day of high tension in the province, as Protestants celebrate the victory of William of Orange over the Catholic King James II in the Battle of the Boyne in 1690 – they carried out another Mk 15 mortar attack on a helicopter.

Their target this time was Puma XW225 of 230 Squadron. As it took off from the Newtownhamilton base in the morning, with eleven soldiers and an RUC officer onboard, a Mk 15 barrack buster was fired, again from a tractor, parked next to a bar in Dundalk Street. 'We felt an explosion of some description next to the aircraft,' explained the pilot. The mortar narrowly missed the Puma, exploding just metres away. 'It almost blew me off my feet,' remarked James Savage, a local councillor, who was in his home nearby when the blast occurred.[22] But the aircraft was peppered with shrapnel from the exploding barrack buster: 'The a/c was damaged in the area of the tail and a fire started,' revealed the Squadron ORB.[23]

'I immediately checked that the aircraft was still flyable, which at that point it was,' recalled the pilot. 'We continued to fly the aircraft away from the town, looking for a clearer area to put down.' Avoiding two residential streets and a school, the pilot carried out an emergency landing on the town's football pitch after losing tail rotor control, part of the undercarriage collapsing as the Puma came down hard. 'She unfortunately then rolled over,' he explained. Its spinning main rotor blades then broke apart as they smashed into the ground. 'But we cushioned it as best we could and the aircraft then came to a standstill fairly rapidly and in not too bad shape, really, considering the blades were broken,' the pilot continued.[24]

Shaken but otherwise uninjured, 'The crew and the 12 passengers onboard evacuated the a/c and managed to extinguish the small fire burning in the tail section,' the ORB disclosed. It was later found that the Puma had been hit by no fewer than seventeen pieces of shrapnel.

Once again, the security forces and the local civilian population had narrowly escaped death or serious injury, something the 230 Squadron ORB attributed to the skill and clear thinking of the pilot: 'The successful landing, following tail rotor drive failure, was well executed and it was only the starboard undercarriage collapsing on landing which caused further damage.'[25]

The pilot was later awarded the third and final DFC of Operation BANNER, for what Army commanders described as his 'great courage' in avoiding the school and putting the crippled helicopter down on the football pitch without serious injury to crew or passengers.

As with the downing of the Lynx in March the attack came in for strong criticism from local community leaders. Cardinal Cahal Daly, the Archbishop of Armagh, condemned the perpetrators for the 'appalling risk of innocent lives that could have been taken if the helicopter had crashed in a built-up area'.[26]

Puma XW225 was later airlifted to Aldergrove by Chinook, where the damage sustained was assessed as Category 3. It was flown by RAF

Hercules to Odiham in England for repairs and returned to service four months later, but was finally written off after crashing during a training exercise in Germany in 1997.

For helicopter crews serving in South Armagh in 1994, Bandit Country was certainly living up to its fearsome reputation. But Puma XW225 was to be the last aircraft brought down by hostile action during the 'Troubles'.

The IRA ceasefire was now just weeks away.

Chapter Ten

Towards Peace

At 1800 hours on 2 June 1994 an RAF Chinook of No. 7 Squadron crashed on the Mull of Kintyre in south-west Scotland. The helicopter had taken off eighteen minutes earlier from RAF Aldergrove on a flight to Fort George, an Army base in Inverness, where its twenty-five passengers, all senior members of the Northern Ireland intelligence community, from the Army, MI5 and RUC Special Branch, were due to attend a security conference. All twenty-five onboard, along with the Chinook's four-man crew, perished in the crash, one of the worst peacetime disasters in the RAF's history.

When news of the crash reached HQNI in Lisburn there were initial fears that the Chinook may have been hit by PIRA fire as it crossed the County Antrim coast on its journey across the Irish Sea to Scotland. 'The suggestion that this Chinook might have taken ground fire caused an instant panic at high level,' an unnamed security source revealed six years later.[1] However, the investigation into the crash ruled out the possibility that the Chinook had either been hit by a SAM or brought down by a bomb planted on board, the accident report stating that 'no evidence of explosive effects or pre-impact fire was found' in the wreckage.[2]

With terrorism ruled out, pilot error was controversially blamed for the accident, though after a high-profile campaign led by the crew's families, several senior politicians and retired military officers, this verdict was later overturned. No definitive cause of the accident has ever been established, though at the time of the crash there were concerns over the reliability of the Chinook.

The tragedy on Kintyre didn't interfere with secret negotiations then underway between British officials and the PIRA leadership, and later that summer the Provisionals released a statement announcing that, from midnight on 31 August, there would be 'a complete cessation of military operations'.

For the next seventeen months there followed an uneasy peace in Northern Ireland. But unlike the 1975 ceasefire, this time there were few serious breaches and 1995 became the first year since the beginning of the 'Troubles' in which there were no security forces' deaths attributable to terrorist violence.

In South Armagh one manifestation of the new, calmer atmosphere was a reduction in military helicopter activity as the Army adopted a lower profile, something which came as a relief to long-suffering locals. 'Before the ceasefire, helicopters were taking off every three minutes,' said one Bessbrook resident. 'There is a quietness in the air and I would like that to last and not be going back to what it was for the past twenty-five years.'[3]

However, those hopes were dashed in February 1996 when PIRA, frustrated at what it regarded as a lack of political progress in negotiations with the British government, which had stalled over the issue of decommissioning of terrorist arms, called off its ceasefire in spectacular fashion by setting off a massive 1,300kg bomb in London's Docklands – constructed and transported to England by members of the South Armagh brigade – which killed two, injured more than a hundred others and caused around £80 million of damage. The Docklands bomb was followed by a resumption of the campaign of violence in Northern Ireland, and for aircrews based in South Armagh it was back to business as usual.

The main threat during the post-ceasefire period came from the notorious South Armagh Sniper, armed with the formidable Barrett M82 'Light Fifty' rifle. Measuring 145 centimetres in length and weighing fourteen kilograms, the Barrett has an effective range of around one and a half kilometres and its fifty calibre bullets can slice through over half-an-inch of steel armour.

The Provisional IRA acquired at least one of these devastating rifles from an arms dealer in the US and succeeded in smuggling it back to Ireland around 1989. Throughout the 1990s the South Armagh Sniper, as he became known, caused considerable alarm among soldiers and policemen with his deadly sniping attacks with the rifle, claiming the lives of five soldiers and one RUC constable (with another seriously wounded), between 1992 and 1997. The number of casualties inflicted was out of all proportion to the fear generated, due to the fact that the Barrett's rounds could easily penetrate the body armour and strengthened helmets worn by troops, and the extreme range from which the sniper could carry out his attacks, which usually left patrols powerless to react.

The sniper was in fact a team of South Armagh brigade members, described by RUC Detective Superintendent Neville McCoubrey as 'one of the most vicious and callous ever put together by the IRA',[4] who carried out one of their attacks from a Mazda car, the sniper firing from the prone position through a hidden panel cut into the boot lid.

The first attack with the Barrett was carried out in March 1990, but it wasn't until 28 August 1992 that the team killed a soldier, Private Paul Turner of the 2nd Bn Light Infantry being cut down whilst on foot patrol in Crossmaglen. The sniper team was most active in the second half of 1993, during which time they killed three soldiers and an RUC constable, and also tried to hit HMS *Cygnet*, the Royal Navy's patrol boat on Carlingford Lough. Their success led to a re-examination of patrolling tactics, with troops coming to rely even more heavily than before on helicopter support. 'For a period, overt patrols only operated under top cover from at least two helicopters,' revealed the Army's official analysis of Operation BANNER.[5] To further minimize risks, when VCPs had to be set up soldiers would often rope down directly onto the road from helicopters.

While these tactics did lead to a sharp drop in sniper activity in South Armagh, the increased reliance on helicopters 'fixed security forces to some extent, and placed a greater burden on the usage of helicopter hours'.[6] Indeed, by 1994 South Armagh was said to account for a third of all hours flown by British military helicopters.[7] To ease the burden on the hard-pressed Support Helicopter Force in South Armagh a detachment of three Sea King HC4s of 846 Naval Air Squadron was despatched to Northern Ireland in April 1994.

But the Barrett Light Fifty was also a highly effective anti-helicopter weapon – a single round from the Barrett could easily bring down a Lynx or a Gazelle. Fortunately, however, the South Armagh Sniper team never used the Barrett rifle against a helicopter. Past experience had shown that large, heavy weapons often had to be abandoned during such attacks, and, possessing just one of the rifles, it's likely PIRA judged the Barrett too valuable and prestigious a weapon to risk losing in a helicopter shoot.

The sniper team's reign of terror finally came to an end in April 1997. Two months earlier they had claimed their sixth and final victim – and, indeed, the final British Army fatality before the resumption of PIRA's interrupted ceasefire – when Lance Bombardier Stephen Restorick of 3rd Regiment Royal Horse Artillery was killed at a checkpoint in Bessbrook. On the morning of 10 April the four-man sniper team – Michael Caraher, Bernard McGinn, Martin Mines and Seamus McArdle – was gathered in a barn on a Cullyhanna farm, preparing another attack on a foot patrol, when sixteen SAS soldiers who had been lying in wait sprang out from their hidden positions. McGinn, Mines and McArdle were captured after a brief struggle but Caraher, believed to be the leader of the team, tried to escape on foot. He was tracked by a Lynx that suddenly appeared overhead, its crew directing the pursuing SAS men to the fleeing target, and was soon captured. A search by the RUC of an animal trailer the next day uncovered the feared Barrett rifle in a hidden compartment. The four suspects were convicted and received sentences ranging from twenty years to life imprisonment, although under the terms of the Belfast Agreement they served only a fraction of their sentences.

It had been a textbook SAS operation, almost certainly based on high-grade informer intelligence and covert aerial surveillance, which was described by some insiders as the Regiment's greatest single blow against the South Armagh IRA.[8]

Just three months after the neutralization of the South Armagh Sniper team, and with its armed campaign throughout the province waning, on 19 July 1997 PIRA released a statement announcing 'the unequivocal restoration of the ceasefire of August 1994'. This time, it would hold.

A new threat

The reinstatement of the ceasefire at first brought little reduction in the military presence in South Armagh, and local people were soon complaining about the continued high level of military aircraft activity in the region. Responding to these complaints, in November the Chief Constable of the RUC, Ronnie Flanagan, explained: 'The threat presented to us and the public in South Armagh is of a very different nature [to that elsewhere in Northern Ireland], so that brings about a different response from us and a different pace in change to that response.'[9]

That threat emanated from dissident republican terrorist groups opposed to the peace process, of which the so-called Real IRA was the largest and most active. Consisting mostly of disillusioned former members of PIRA, several of them from South Armagh, the group was formed in November 1997 by Michael McKevitt, the Provisionals' former 'Quartermaster General' from Dundalk. The group came to international prominence in August 1998 after setting off a car bomb in the centre of Omagh, killing thirty-one civilians (among them a woman pregnant with twins) – the deadliest single attack of the 'Troubles' – five months after the signing of the Belfast Agreement seemed to herald a new era of peace and stability for the province.

Despite the universal condemnation that greeted this horrific atrocity, after briefly standing down the Real IRA resumed its campaign of terrorism in January 2000. Though much smaller than PIRA and possessing far fewer weapons, the group has maintained a low-level terror campaign ever since. Of the continuing dissident republican threat, the Independent Monitoring Commission, which observed the ceasefire in Northern Ireland, reported in 2006: 'Their capacity for sustained campaigns is limited but they are prepared to resort to extreme violence. The threat they pose is higher in some places, of which South Armagh is the most obvious'.[10]

It was reported that the Real IRA's centre of operations was Forkhill, and a sizeable proportion of their attacks have taken place in South Armagh. Within months of PIRA reinstating its ceasefire, the RUC had begun tentatively using the roads again in the region, for the first time in more than twenty years. The Real IRA's response was to detonate a large landmine on 22 June 1998 near Drumintee, cratering the Newry-Forkhill Road, which was seen as a warning to the security forces that they shouldn't assume they could now patrol the roads of South Armagh with impunity.

But while the roads were still dangerous, the skies remained relatively safe, the dissidents being unable to emulate the now defunct South Armagh brigade's offensive against helicopters, probably due to the group's lack of heavy weaponry.

To remedy this, a group of Real IRA members travelled to several European cities with a 'shopping list' of weapons they wished to procure from an arms dealer known as 'Ali', including 12.7mm HMGs and SA-7 Strela SAMs. However, in an echo of the classic FBI sting operations of the 1980s that thwarted the Provos' efforts to acquire Redeyes and Stingers, the Real IRA team were being lured into a trap laid by MI5. In June 2006 three suspects were arrested, all of whom were from County Armagh, and two were later convicted. Five years later, a second MI5 undercover sting, codenamed Operation UNCRITICAL, prevented another dissident republican plot to buy black market arms in Lithuania, including a Harris M96 .50 calibre sniper rifle, similar to the Barrett Light Fifty.

Defeated in their attempts to add shoulder-launched SAMs to their armoury, the dissidents then tried to replicate the Provisionals' success using homemade mortars against helicopters. In August 2013 the PSNI received a report of an unexploded bomb in the village of Cullyhanna. Suspecting a 'come-on', intended to lure them into an ambush, the police held off. Their suspicions were well-founded, for a follow-up search in a wooded area unearthed two mortars, abandoned by the terrorists, which it was believed they intended to use to shoot down a Eurocopter EC145 of the PSNI's Air Support Unit as it responded to the bogus bomb threat.

The mortars were made safe by an Army EOD team. The apparent sophistication of the devices, which it was reported were to be triggered either by mobile phone signal or infra-red laser, reportedly surprised the security forces and led to speculation that the dissidents had gained knowledge from foreign guerrilla armies, such as the Taliban in Afghanistan. 'When it comes to the sophistication, when it comes to the technological detail, these are things that have never been seen in Northern Ireland,' said a Unionist MP.[11] A Real IRA splinter group was blamed for the aborted attack.

From BANNER to HELVETIC

The continuing activities of dissident republicans notwithstanding, the more settled political environment in the province and the announcement by PIRA in July 2005 that they had now put their arms beyond use allowed the British military to steadily scale down its presence in Northern Ireland, including reducing helicopter flying hours. Whereas in June 2004 flying hours throughout the province for that month had totalled 1,651, by January 2006 this was down to 766 hours.[12]

By then the Wessex had already disappeared from Ulster's skies: 72 Squadron having been disbanded in April 2002. This was followed in March 2007 with the standing down of the AAC's 655 Squadron.

The last major air operation carried out in South Armagh was airlifting out the dismantled sections of the Golf and Romeo watchtowers, which had been such a bone of contention between the military and the nationalist community during the 'Troubles'. Due to local sensitivities over British troops on the ground and the continuing IED threat on the roads, the dismantled installations were removed entirely by air, using Pumas and Chinooks, in a massive programme codenamed Operation SADDLERY. 'We've got to airlift everything out,' confirmed Colonel Wayne Harber, deputy commander of 39 Infantry Brigade, in 2006. 'Every portakabin, every nail, every screw, piece of concrete - every pebble of gravel has got to be airlifted out.'[13] Operation SADDLERY was completed in February 2007 with the removal of the last military installation in South Armagh, a guard post in Crossmaglen.

Nothing symbolized the end of the military's role in Bandit Country more than the closure of Bessbrook Mill on 25 June 2007. Three days before, the last aircraft had left the base, a Royal Navy Lynx HAS3 of 815 Naval Air Squadron ORU (Operational Readiness Unit). 'The closure of Bessbrook is significant because it is our last base in South Armagh, which has always been an area of particular operational interest,' General Sir Nick Parker, the GOC Northern Ireland said of the occasion.[14]

The last helicopter lost in South Armagh during Operation BANNER was Lynx ZD276 of 655 Squadron, which crashed due to bad weather in Crossmaglen on 18 March 2007, injuring two AAC crewmen and the four PSNI officers it was transporting.

On 25 July 2007 a low-key statement by the Defence Minister Bob Ainsworth announcing the formal conclusion of Operation BANNER the following week was read out in Parliament:

> On 31 July, Operation BANNER will come to an end; the Army, Royal Air Force and Royal Navy having delivered continuous support to the police and civil authorities in Northern Ireland for 38 years. It will have been the longest continuous deployment of UK Armed Forces in their history.

The much reduced Army garrison in the province would, however, retain limited responsibilities in support of the PSNI, this support role going under the name Operation HELVETIC. 'Military helicopters,' Ainsworth's statement went on, 'will continue to be based in Northern Ireland ... in support of the civil authorities.'[15] As part of Operation HELVETIC, the AAC continues to provide airborne surveillance, with several Gazelles of 665 Squadron and the Islanders of 1 Flight, 651 Squadron stationed at RAF Aldergrove, which became Joint Helicopter Command Flying Station Aldergrove after the departure of the RAF's last unit, 230 Squadron, in 2009.

Ainsworth's statement concluded with a tribute to 'the commitment, bravery and sacrifice of all those who have served over so many years in helping to deliver the current more settled and more optimistic circumstances'.

Operation BANNER: an analysis of the air war

The contribution of airmen and ground crews of the three services to Operation BANNER was immense. The Army Air Corps alone flew over 700,000 hours on counter-terrorism operations during the conflict, losing twenty-four aircraft to all causes (plus one from the Royal Marines' 3 CBAS). In 2006 the Corps was awarded the prestigious Barnes Wallis Medal in recognition of its 'exceptional contribution to NI military operations on land, at sea and in the air over the past 37 years,' with the citation pointing out that the AAC had made 'a substantial contribution to operations in which terrorists were captured, Improvised Explosive Devices discovered and defused, and military and civilian casualties evacuated, in addition to the routine activities of daily life in the province'.

The citation also highlighted the AAC's pioneering use of new equipment in Northern Ireland, including 'Heli-Tele' surveillance cameras and Night Vision Goggles, of which AAC units in Northern Ireland 'were the first to employ for front-line operational flying duties'.

The contribution of the RAF's Support Helicopter Force, equipped with medium-lift Wessex and Pumas, and later the heavy-lift Chinooks of 7 Squadron, was hardly any less impressive. As an example, from its arrival in the province as a permanent presence in 1992 until the end of BANNER, 230 Squadron flew over 37,000 operational hours, and twenty-six of its personnel were awarded honours and decorations (among which were fourteen Queen's Commendations for Valuable Service in the Air and the RAF's only DFC of the conflict).[16] Seven RAF aircraft crashed in Northern Ireland, only one of which was brought down by enemy action.

While often overlooked, the Royal Navy's involvement was also significant. In addition to their main role during the 'Troubles' of patrolling the waters around Northern Ireland to interdict the movement of weapons and terrorists by boat, the Wessex and Sea Kings of 845 and 846 Naval Air Squadrons periodically deployed to South Armagh from 1977 onwards to support the Army and RAF helicopter fleet during periods of over-stretch. RN aircrew were also seconded to the RAF and AAC. Neither should the involvement of the Royal Marines' 3 Commando Brigade Air Squadron be ignored. Equipped first with the Sioux, and from 1976 with the Gazelle, Royal Marine airmen served in the province from the very beginning of the 'Troubles', the first to arrive being Lieutenant Andrew Eames, who was serving as an exchange pilot with 8 Flight AAC when it deployed to Northern Ireland in August 1969.

Among the flying awards conferred on airmen in Operation BANNER were one DFM, three DFCs, all of which were awarded for acts of gal-lantry that took place in South Armagh, five AFMs and twenty-three AFCs, along with scores of MiDs and Queen's Commendations.

All these achievements did not come without cost. According to the official figures, 763 British military personnel were killed as a result of terrorism during Operation BANNER, 127 of those in South Armagh. Twenty-six RAF personnel (including members of the RAF Regiment) and seventeen soldiers serving with the Army Air Corps lost their lives to all causes. However, only two pilots were killed by terrorist action.[17] No aircrew were killed in the air by IRA ground fire, though around a dozen were injured.

The war in South Armagh also provided crews with operational expe-rience in a long, drawn-out counter-insurgency campaign that would prove invaluable in the subsequent conflicts in which British forces would become embroiled in the twenty-first century. 'At the time, flying in Northern Ireland was very demanding for all pilots, especially inex-perienced ones, as I was,' explained Lieutenant Commander Graeme Spence, who flew Sea King HC4s with 846 NAS in South Armagh in the 1990s. 'Although I didn't know it then, but I learnt so many skills in that environment that I would subsequently rely on in later years, both in Iraq and Afghanistan.'[18]

And what of the chief antagonists, PIRA's South Armagh bri-gade? Their most significant strategic success during the conflict was undoubtedly in forcing the Army off the roads and into the air with their roadside bombing campaign of the 1970s. While the press and many British officers considered the relinquishing of the roads to be a humiliation and evidence that 'the Queen's writ has ceased to run in the border areas of County Armagh', as one British politician put it, others felt that the forced reliance on air transport was ultimately beneficial, encouraging the Army to develop 'a genuinely airmobile concept of operations in South Armagh and several other places,' according to the Army's official analysis of Operation BANNER. Helicopters, it added, 'gave the security forces a considerable advantage through operational mobility.'[19]

However, this heavy dependence on helicopters could have proven to be the security forces' Achilles heel, as it had the Americans in Vietnam and the Soviets in Afghanistan, had PIRA's anti-aircraft offensive been more successful. In both the US intervention in Vietnam and the Soviet-Afghan War of the 1980s, heavy helicopter losses to guerrilla ground fire was a major factor in forcing the world's two superpowers to withdraw from those countries.[20]

The war in Northern Ireland was, of course, on a tiny scale in comparison to those two conflicts. Even so, PIRA were never able to replicate anything like the success the Viet Cong and mujahedeen enjoyed against the airpower deployed by their enemies. Between 1974, when their anti-aircraft offensive began in earnest, until the end of the 'Troubles' in the late 1990s, over thirty-five recorded attacks were mounted against British military aircraft in South Armagh, with a much smaller number in the border areas of Tyrone and Fermanagh. Only six helicopters were brought down by hostile fire (three of which were repairable and eventually returned to service), with a further nine suffering serious damage and around a dozen light to moderate damage from enemy fire. The remainder of the helicopters lost during Operation BANNER were as a result of pilot error, bad weather or mechanical failure.

Nevertheless, the re-arming of PIRA by Colonel Gaddafi in the mid-1980s, and their subsequent deployment of powerful weapons such as the Dushka 12.7mm HMG, presented an entirely new level of threat to air operations in the border areas, forcing the British to respond by arming helicopters and flying in pairs to provide mutual support. These changes in tactics 'severely inhibited the ability of the terrorist to get away,' insisted the Army's analysis of Operation BANNER.[21]

The enormous effort PIRA invested in acquiring shoulder-launched SAMs also brought little result. US law enforcement agencies successfully infiltrated and dismantled all of their plots to get hold of these potentially war-winning weapons in America. And while they did eventually receive several SA-7s from Gaddafi, the single occasion in which one was used against a British helicopter in Northern Ireland (in Fermanagh in July 1991) was a failure.

Though they gave senior British military commanders a few scares, particularly during the period 1988-1994, ultimately their campaign against aircraft lacked cohesion and they failed in their stated aim to halt movement by air in South Armagh.

Today, the heavily fortified watchtowers that once scarred the land-scape and incessant drone of helicopters that filled the air are increas-ingly a distant memory, and South Armagh is even re-inventing itself as a tourist destination.

For British airmen who served there during the height of the violence, the transformation of the place known to them as Bandit Country has been nothing short of remarkable. 'Crossmaglen, in my time, was a place I would never have set foot on the ground,' said retired RAF pilot Mike Johnston, whose Wessex was badly damaged in an RPG and machine-gun attack in Crossmaglen in April 1976. In 2015, now a civilian, he returned to the town where so many soldiers and policemen lost their lives during the 'Troubles' and witnessed first-hand the dramatic changes the area had undergone. 'And I reflected on that and thought, "Well, this place has moved on tremendously." I think peace is slowly coming across.'[22]

Aircraft crashes/forced landings in South Armagh during Operation BANNER

Type	Serial	Sqn	Date	Location	Details
Sioux	XW195	652	18/12/75	Crossmaglen	Hit power lines.
Scout	XV133	662	7/1/76	Crossmaglen	Crashed flying in low cloud. Pilot, WO2 Brian Jackson, and Corporal Arthur Ford killed.
Gazelle	XX404	657	17/2/78	Jonesborough	Crashed after coming under hostile fire. Lt Col Ian Corden-Lloyd killed.
Scout	XW614	659	2/12/78	Lough Ross	Crashed during night-time sortie. Captain Allan Stirling and Corporal Roger Adcock killed.
Gazelle	XZ293	662	24/8/79	Jerrettspass	Hit power lines. L/Cpl David Lang and L/Cpl David Wares killed.
Gazelle	XX400	655	1/12/82	Crossmaglen	Hit power lines.
Wessex	XT669	72	25/10/85	Forkhill	Crashed after main rotors hit radio mast during night take-off. Air Loadmaster Sgt Dave Rigby killed.
Lynx	XZ664	665	23/6/88	Silverbridge	Force-landed after being hit by hostile fire.
Lynx	ZE380	665	13/2/91	Crossmaglen	Force-landed after being hit by hostile fire.
Gazelle	ZB681	665	26/11/92	Bessbrook	Collided with Puma XW233 when coming in to land at Bessbrook Mill.

Type	Serial	Sqn	Date	Location	Details
Puma	XW233	230	26/11/92	Bessbrook	Collided with Gazelle ZB681. Sqn Ldr Michael Haverson, Flt Lt Simon Roberts, Flt Sgt Jan Pewtress and Major John Barr killed.
Lynx	ZD275	655	19/3/94	Crossmaglen	Destroyed after being hit by PIRA mortar.
Puma	XW225	230	12/7/94	Newtown-hamilton	Force-landed after being damaged by PIRA mortar.
Lynx	XZ662	655	2/3/00	Mullaghbawn	Badly damaged in heavy landing.
Puma	XW227	230	16/3/02	Jonesborough	Crashed on hilltop landing site.
Lynx	ZD276	655	18/3/07	Crossmaglen	Crashed in bad weather.

Aircraft types operated by AAC, RN and RAF during Operation BANNER

Westland Sioux AH1
Type: Liaison and observation helicopter
Operators: Army Air Corps, 3 CBAS
BANNER Years of Service: 1969–77
Powerplant: 1 x Avco Lycoming engine
Performance: Maximum speed 105mph/169km/h.
Capacity: 2 crew and 1 passenger
Armament: None (1 x 7.62 mm GPMG on trials only)

Westland Scout AH1
Type: Light transport and general utility helicopter
Operators: Army Air Corps, 3 CBAS
BANNER Years of Service: 1969–82
Powerplant: 1 x Rolls-Royce Nimbus turboshaft engine
Performance: Maximum speed 130 mph/210km/h
Capacity: 2 crew and 4 troops
Armament: None (2 x 7.62 mm GPMGs on trials only)

Westland Wessex HC2/HU5
Type: Medium-lift troop transport, general utility and SAR (search and rescue) helicopter
Operators: RAF, Royal Navy
BANNER Years of Service: 1969–2002 (HC2)/1977–1982 (HU5)
Powerplant: 2 x de Havilland Gnome turboshaft engines
Performance: Maximum speed 132mph/213km/h
Capacity: 3 crew and 16 troops
Armament: 1 x 7.62 mm GPMG (from 1990 onwards)

Westland Puma HC1
Type: Medium-lift troop transport and general utility helicopter

Operator: RAF
BANNER Years of Service: 1972–2007
Powerplant: 2 x Turbomeca turboshaft engines
Performance: Maximum speed 169mph/273km/h
Capacity: 3 crew and 16 troops
Armament: 1 x 7.62 mm GPMG (from 1990 onwards)

de Havilland-Canada DHC-2 Beaver AL1
Type: Fixed-wing reconnaissance aircraft
Operator: Army Air Corps
BANNER Years of Service: 1973–89
Powerplant: 1 x Pratt & Whitney R-985 Wasp Jnr radial engine
Performance: Maximum speed 158mph/254km/h
Capacity: 6 passengers and crew
Armament: None

BAe Canberra PR 9
Type: High-altitude, twin-jet photo-reconnaissance aircraft
Operator: RAF
BANNER Years of Service: Unknown
Powerplant: 2 x Rolls-Royce Avon turbojets
Performance: Maximum speed 580mph/933km/h
Armament: None

Aérospatiale SA 341 Gazelle AH1
Type: Liaison, observation and surveillance helicopter
Operator: Army Air Corps, 3 CBAS
BANNER Years of Service: 1976–2007
Powerplant: 1 x Turbomeca Astazou IIIA turboshaft engine
Performance: Maximum speed 193mph/310km/h
Capacity: 2 crew and 3 passengers
Armament: None

Westland Lynx AH1/AH7/HAS 3
Type: Light/medium troop transport and general utility helicopter
Operator: Army Air Corps, Royal Navy

BANNER Years of Service: 1979-2007
Powerplant: 2 x Rolls-Royce Gem turboshaft engines
Performance: 205mph/330km/h
Capacity: 2 crew (later, 3 with addition of door gunner) and 9 troops
Armament: 1 x 7.62 mm GPMG (from 1990 onwards)

Boeing Chinook HC2
Type: Heavy-lift transport helicopter
Operator: RAF
BANNER Years of Service: 1988-2007
Powerplant: 2 x Textron Lycoming turboshaft engines
Performance: Maximum speed 183mph/295km/h
Capacity: 3/4 crew and 55 troops
Armament: None

Britten-Norman Islander AL1
Type: General transport, photo-reconnaissance and electronic surveillance aircraft
Operators: Army Air Corps
BANNER Years of Service: 1989-2007
Powerplant: 2 x Rolls-Royce Allison turboprop engines
Performance: Maximum speed 170mph/273km/h
Capacity: 10 passengers and crew
Armament: None

Westland Sea King HC4
Type: Medium-lift troop transport and general utility helicopter
Operator: Royal Navy
BANNER Years of Service: 1994-99
Powerplant: 2 x Rolls-Royce Gnome turboshaft engines
Performance: Maximum speed 129mph/208km/h
Capacity: 3 crew and 28 troops
Armament: 1 x 7.62mm GPMG

End Notes

Introduction
1. Taylor, *Provos: The IRA and Sinn Fein*, p. 3
2. *Operation Banner: An Analysis of British Military Operations in Northern Ireland*

Chapter One: Troubled Times
1. Omissi, *Air Power and Colonial Control: The RAF 1919-1939*, p. 42
2. Sheehan, *British Voices from the Irish War of Independence 1918-21*, p.61
3. National Archives, Kew, WO 141/44, Memo from Trenchard, 9 October 1920
4. Gilbert, *Churchill: A Life*, p. 422
5. Sheehan, op. cit., p. 151
6. Witness Statement: 0932, www.bureauofmilitaryhistory.ie
7. *Flight*, 19 August 1920
8. Witness Statement: 600, www.bureauofmilitaryhistory.ie
9. *Irish Times*, 8 September 1958
10. Imperial War Museum sound archive (tape number: 33894)
11. Wragg, *Helicopters At War*, p. 112
12. *Handbook for Volunteers of the IRA: Notes on Guerrilla Warfare*, p. 28
13. Warner, *Sycamores Over Ulster*, p. 31
14. National Archives, Kew, AIR 27/2705, Operations Record Book (ORB), 118 Squadron, February 1960
15. Ibid.
16. The airmen killed in the two Auster crashes were Captain Cracknell, Staff Sergeant Hall and Flight Lieutenant Readman
17. Warner, op. cit., p. 52
18. National Archives, Kew, CAB 129/144/7, Memo by Minister of Defence for Administration Roy Hattersley, 28 July 1969

Chapter Two: Bandit Country aka 'The Independent Republic of South Armagh'

1. National Archives, Kew, PREM 19/280, South Armagh Area Review, 2 April 1980
2. Dillon, *The Dirty War*, p. 167
3. *Irish Times*, 22 January 1985
4. *The Guardian*, 17 December 1975
5. Parry, *Down South: A Falklands War Diary*, p. 28
6. *Belfast Newsletter*, 9 November 2011
7. Harnden, *Bandit Country The IRA & South Armagh*, p. 115
8. *The Guardian*, 17 December 1975
9. Public Record Office of Northern Ireland, Belfast, CENT 1/5/5, NIO memo 'Paramilitary organisation in Northern Ireland', 13 February 1976
10. National Archives Ireland, Dublin, reference: 2005/7/664, Memo from Merlyn Rees to Garret FitzGerald, 19 December 1974
11. National Archives, Kew, CAB 129/181, Defence estimates statement, 25 February 1975
12. *Irish Times*, 24 November 1975
13. *The Guardian*, 4 January 1976
14. This was not, however, the Regiment's first involvement in the 'Troubles'. In September 1969, D Squadron SAS was briefly sent to Northern Ireland to search for terrorist arms, while elements of B Squadron were deployed in a limited surveillance role in 1974.
15. Harnden, op. cit., p. 68
16. *Irish Times*, 20 November 1982
17. National Archives, Kew, PREM 19/279, MoD memo, 10 January 1980
18. *Irish Times*, 30 June 2009
19. *Hansard*, 12 January 1976
20. Bailey, Iron and Strachan (editors), *British Generals in Blair's Wars*, p. 30

Chapter Three: 'Everything was done by helicopter'

1. Imperial War Museum sound archive (tape number: 28361)
2. Arthur, *Northern Ireland: Soldiers Talking*, p. 178
3. *Navy News*, September 2007
4. Warner, *Army Aviation in Ulster*, p. 72

5. National Archives, Kew, AIR 27/3454, Operations Record Book (ORB),72 Squadron, August 1979

6. McNab, *Immediate Action*, p. 23 (reproduced by permission of The Random House Group Ltd. © 1995)

7. Imperial War Museum sound archive (tape number: 33200)

8. *Daily Express*, 25 August 1979

9. National Archives, Kew, AIR 27/3685, Report on Support Helicopter Force Northern Ireland, 6 June 1983

10. National Archives, Kew, WO 373/183, Recommendation for award of Air Force Cross, 12 March 1990

11. Jackson, *Soldier*, p. 152

12. *Irish Times*, 8 July 1980

13. *We Were There* (British Forces Broadcasting Service, broadcast 12 May 2015)

14. National Archives, Kew, AIR 27/3454, Operations Record Book (ORB), 72 Squadron, August 1979

15. Army incident report, 31 January 1976

16. *Hansard*, 22 November 1979

17. Irish parliamentary debate, 13 May 1976

18. Irish parliamentary debate, 18 October 1973

19. Imperial War Museum sound archive (tape number: 33735)

20. *Irish Times*, 23 January 2009

21. National Archives Ireland, Dublin, Memorandum by Merlyn Rees to Garret FitzGerald, 19 December 1974

22. National Archives Ireland, Dublin, Report: 'British Request for Permission to Overfly', 4 May 1973

23. *Flight International*, 6 January 1972 (reproduced with permission of Reed Business Information Limited via PLSClear)

24. *The Guardian*, 12 April 2002

Chapter Four: Pot-shots

1. Warner, *First in the Field: 651 Squadron Army Air Corps*, p. 153

2. Imperial War Museum sound archive (tape number: 33200)

3. Moloney, *Voices from the Grave: Two Men's War in Ireland*, p. 86

4. Hostile Action Report, dated 13 January 1972

5. Imperial War Museum sound archive (tape number: 33200)

6. Warner, op. cit., pp. 151–2

7. Hostile Action Report, dated 14 December 1972

8. McKittrick, et al, *Lost Lives*, p. 359

9. www.flyingmarines.com

10. Ibid.

11. National Archives, Kew, DEFE 24/1945, Memo: 'Armed helicopters in Northern Ireland', 28 March 1973

12. Stone, *Cold War Warriors*, p. 185

13. National Archives, Kew, DEFE 24/1945, Memo: 'Armed helicopters in Northern Ireland', 28 March 1973

14. National Archives, Kew, DEFE 24/1945, 'Northern Ireland: use of helicopters'

15. Ibid.

16. Ibid.

17. Ibid.

18. *Der Spiegel*, 19 November 1973

19. *Women Of The IRA* (TG4 documentary, broadcast 5 January 2012)

20. *Irish Times*, 25 January 1974

21. National Archives, Kew, DEFE 24/1945, 'Northern Ireland: use of helicopters'

22. *Irish Independent* and *Irish Press*, 30 September 1974

Chapter Five: Priority Target

1. McGuire, *Enemy of the Empire*, p. 243

2. Author's correspondence with 38 (Irish) Brigade, 15 April 2016

3. Harnden, *Bandit Country The IRA & South Armagh*, p. 68

4. Ashcroft, *Heroes of the Skies*, pp 393–5 (© 2012 MAA Publishing Limited. Reproduced by permission of Headline Publishing Group)

5. Ibid. p. 396

6. BBC Radio Ulster, 5 January 2016

7. Ibid.

8. Clarke, *Contact*, p. 103

9. Spencer, *Air Force Records: A Guide for Family Historians*, p. 99

10. Imperial War Museum sound archive (tape number: 30108)

11. Board of Inquiry report into crash of Gazelle XX404, 18 March 1978

12. Ibid.

13. Ibid.
14. *Hansard*, 21 February 1978
15. *Hansard*, 6 March 1978
16. *Hansard*, 20 February 1978
17. *Flight International*, 16 December 1978
18. Board of Inquiry report into crash of Gazelle XX404, 18 March 1978
19. Ibid.
20. Halstock, *Rats The Story of a Dog Soldier*, pp. 50–1
21. *Hansard*, 25 July 1979
22. Harnden, op. cit., p. 208
23. National Archives, Kew, PREM 19/82, Memo from Humphrey Atkins to PM, 5 October 1979
24. National Archives, Kew, PREM 19/82, Memo from NIO to PM, 10 October 1979
25. *Irish Times*, 10 November 1979
26. Army Incident Report, HQNI, 10 September 1979
27. Army Incident Report, HQNI, 7 May 1981

Chapter Six: 'If it flies, it dies' The SAM Threat
1. Glover, *Future Terrorist Trends*
2. Taylor, *Provos The IRA and Sinn Fein*, p. 3
3. Ibid. p. 3
4. Bradley and Feeney, *Insider: Gerry Bradley's life in the IRA*, p. 181
5. Army incident report, HQNI, 26 July 1982
6. Ibid.
7. National Archives, Kew, AIR 27/3588, Operations Record Book (ORB), 72 Squadron, July/August 1982
8. Army incident report, HQNI, 26 July 1982
9. National Archives, Kew, AIR 27/3685, Operations Record Book (ORB), 72 Squadron, May 1983
10. Ibid.
11. Ibid.
12. Ibid.
13. Army incident report, HQNI, 24 May 1985
14. Arthur, *Northern Ireland: Soldiers Talking*, p. 200
15. Yousaf and Adkin, *The Battle for Afghanistan*, pp. 174–6

16. Crile, *Charlie Wilson's War*, p. 404
17. Ibid. p. 437
18. Yousaf and Adkin, op. cit., p. 179
19. Braithwaite, *Afgantsy*, p. 204
20. *Sun Sentinel*, 5 December 1990
21. Harnden, *Bandit Country The IRA & South Armagh*, p. 378
22. *Sun Sentinel*, 5 December 1990
23. *Sun Sentinel*, 12 December 1990
24. Imperial War Museum sound archive (tape number: 33200)
25. *Daily Telegraph*, 8 April 2013

Chapter Seven: Gifts from the Colonel

1. Bradley and Feeney, *Insider: Gerry Bradley's Life in the IRA*, pp. 210–11
2. *Hansard*, 30 June 1988
3. www.thebrokenelbow.com
4. O'Brien, *The Long War: The IRA and Sinn Fein 1985 to Today*, p. 138
5. Published figures for the amount of weaponry supplied to PIRA by Colonel Gaddafi vary. In August 1992, during a thaw in Anglo-Libyan relations, it was reported that Tripoli had provided the UK government with full details of the arms shipments sent to Ireland, but these figures have yet to be made public.
6. O'Callaghan, *The Informer*, p. 281
7. *Ulster Herald*, 17 February 1990
8. *Daily Telegraph*, 30 July 2007
9. 72 Squadron Operations Record Book (ORB), January 1991 (via RAF Air Historical Branch)
10. Board of Inquiry report into forced-landing of Lynx ZE380, dated 12 April 1991
11. Ibid.
12. Ibid.
13. *DERR Journal*, February 1991
14. *Irish Times*, 25 February 1991
15. *Irish Times*, 1 April 1991
16. *DERR Journal*, February 1991
17. *An Phoblacht*, August 1991

18. Brigadier Mohammed Yousaf, the Pakistani intelligence chief who liaised with the mujahedeen in Afghanistan, wrote that 'a few flares could usually be relied on to deflect our [SA-7] missiles off course'. Yousaf and Adkin, *The Battle for Afghanistan*, p. 178

19. *Sunday Telegraph*, 15 September 1991

20. Author's correspondence with 38 (Irish) Brigade, 3 March 2017

21. *Irish Press*, 17 March 1992

22. www.jsbni.com

Chapter Eight: Striking Back

1. 72 Squadron Monthly Report, February 1990 (via RAF Air Historical Branch)

2. 72 Squadron Operations Record Book (ORB), February 1990 (via RAF Air Historical Branch)

3. Imperial War Museum sound archive (tape number: 28698)

4. 72 Squadron Operations Record Book (ORB), February 1990

5. *Irish Press*, 22 February 1990

6. 72 Squadron Operations Record Book (ORB), February 1990

7. Imperial War Museum sound archive (tape number: 28698)

8. 72 Squadron Monthly Report, February 1990

9. *Hansard*, 22 June 1989

10. 72 Squadron Operations Record Book (ORB), December 1989 (via RAF air Historical Branch)

11. Author's correspondence with MoD, 7 April 2017

12. Board of Inquiry report into forced-landing of Lynx ZE380, dated 12 April 1991

13. Army incident report, HQNI, 9 January 1993

14. *An Phoblacht*, July 1994

15. Ashcroft, *Heroes of the Skies*, pp. 411–12 (© 2012 MAA Publishing Limited. Reproduced by permission of Headline Publishing Group)

16. Ibid. p. 412

17. Ibid. p. 412

18. *An Phoblacht*, July 1994

19. Ashcroft, op. cit., p. 413

20. Ibid. p. 413

21. *An Phoblacht*, July 1994

22. Imperial War Museum sound archive (tape number: 30025)

23. Rennie, *The Operators*, p. 155

24. Macy, *Hellfire*, p. 57

25. Bradley and Feeney, *Insider: Gerry Bradley's Life in the IRA*, p. 203

26. Harnden, *Bandit Country The IRA & South Armagh*, p. 397

27. 72 Squadron Operations Record Book (ORB), May 1992 (via RAF air Historical Branch)

28. Author's correspondence with PSNI, 11 March 2016

29. *Irish Times*, 16 November 1993

Chapter Nine: Home-Made Solutions

1. Harnden, *Bandit Country The IRA & South Armagh*, pp. 353 and 366

2. *The Morning Call*, 2 May 1990

3. *Irish Echo*, 3 February 1999

4. *Tulsa World*, 15 July 1989

5. *LA Times*, 14 July 1989

6. A similar plan was conceived by the British during the Blitz of 1940-41 to bring down Luftwaffe bombers. Codenamed Operation ALBINO, the results proved disappointing.

7. *The Morning Call*, 17 May 1990

8. Kessler, *The FBI*, p. 383

9. Harnden, op. cit., p. 233

10. Geraghty, *The Irish War*, p. 191

11. National Archives, Kew, AIR 27/3685, Operations Record Book (ORB), 72 Squadron, June 1983

12. Arthur, *Northern Ireland Soldiers Talking*, p. 200

13. *Glasgow Herald*, 17 April 1987

14. Smith, *3-2-1 Bomb Gone*, p. 139

15. 230 Squadron Operations Record Book (ORB), June 1993 (via RAF Air Historical Branch)

16. Wharton, *A Long Long War: Voices from the British Army in Northern Ireland 1969 - 1998*, p. 472

17. *The Guardian*, 21 March 1994

18. Wharton, op. cit., p. 472

19. *The Times*, 21 March 1994

20. Geraghty, op. cit., p. 200

21. *The Independent*, 26 March 1994

22. *Irish Independent*, 13 July 1994

23. 230 Squadron Operations Record Book (ORB), July 1994 (via RAF Air Historical Branch)

24. *Irish Times*, 13 July 1994

25. 230 Squadron Operations Record Book (ORB), July 1994

26. *Irish Times*, 13 July 1994

Chapter Ten: Towards Peace

1. *Glasgow Herald*, 13 December 2000

2. *Hansard*, 31 January 2002

3. *Irish Times*, 24 February 1995

4. Geraghty, *The Irish War*, p. 186

5. *Operation Banner: An Analysis of Military Operations in Northern Ireland*

6. Ibid.

7. Harnden, *Bandit Country The IRA & South Armagh*, p. 405

8. Ibid. p. 354

9. *Irish Times*, 26 November 1997

10. Independent Monitoring Commission, Ninth Report, March 2006

11. *Independent on Sunday*, 1 December 2013

12. Independent Monitoring Commission, Ninth Report, March 2006

13. *Irish Times*, 30 June 2006

14. *The Scotsman*, 26 June 2007

15. *Hansard*, 25 July 2007

16. *Hansard*, 7 May 2008

17. Staff Sergeant Arthur Place and Royal Marine Sergeant Derek Reed, both killed in the Knock-Na-Moe Hotel car bombing on 17 May 1973

18. www.fleetairarmoa.org

19. *Operation Banner: An Analysis of Military Operations in Northern Ireland*

20. The US lost a total of 5,086 rotary-wing aircraft during the Vietnam War, of which over 2,000 were shot down by Viet Cong guerrillas, while the Soviets lost 333 helicopters in their war against the mujahedeen in Afghanistan.

21. *Operation Banner: An Analysis of Military Operations in Northern Ireland*

22. BBC Radio Ulster, 5 January 2016

Bibliography

Books

Adkin, Mark and Yousaf, Muhammed, *The Battle For Afghanistan* (Pen & Sword, 2009)

Arthur, Max, *Northern Ireland: Soldiers Talking* (Sidgwick & Jackson, 1987)

Ashcroft, Michael, *Heroes of The Skies* (Headline, 2012)

Bailey, Jonathan; Iron, Richard; Strachan, Hew (editors), *British Generals in Blair's Wars* (Routledge, 2013)

Bell, J. Bowyer, *The Secret Army: The IRA* (Transaction, 1997)

Braithwaite, Rodric, *Afgantsy* (Profile Books, 2011)

Clarke, A.F.N., *Contact* (Secker & Warburg, 1983)

Dillon, Martin, *The Dirty War* (Arrow, 1991)

Dingley, James (editor), *Combating Terrorism in Northern Ireland* (Routledge, 2008)

Flintham, Vic, *High Stakes: Britain's Air Arms in Action 1945-1990* (Pen & Sword, 2009)

Geraghty, Tony, *The Irish War* (HarperCollins, 1998)

Gilbert, Martin, *Churchill: A Life* (Pimlico, 2000)

Halstock, Max, *Rats: The Story of a Dog Soldier* (Corgi, 1982)

Harnden, Toby, *Bandit Country The IRA & South Armagh* (Hodder, 2000)

Henderson, Tam and Hunt, John, *Warrior: A True Story of Bravery and Betrayal in the Iraq War* (Mainstream, 2008)

Jackson, General Sir Mike, *Soldier* (Corgi, 2008)

Kessler, Ronald, *The FBI* (Corgi, 1994)

Lindsay, Oliver, *Once A Grenadier* (Pen & Sword, 1996)

Macy, Ed, *Hellfire* (Harper Press, 2010)

McGuire, Eamon, *Enemy of The Empire* (The O'Brien Press, 2006)

McNab, Andy, *Immediate Action* (Bantam Press, 1995)

McNulty, Thomas, *Exiled: 40 Years An Exile* (TMN Publications, 2014)

Moloney, Ed, *A Secret History Of The IRA* (Penguin, 2002)

Moloney, Ed (editor), *Voices From The Grave: Two Men's War in Ireland* (Faber & Faber, 2010)

O'Brien, Brendan, *The Long War: The IRA and Sinn Fein 1985 to Today* (Syracuse University Press, 1999)

O'Callaghan, Sean, *The Informer* (Corgi, 1999)

Omissi, David E., *Air Power and Colonial Control: The RAF 1919-1939* (Manchester University Press, 1990)

Parry, Chris, *Down South: A Falklands War Diary* (Viking, 2012)

Rennie, James, *The Operators* (Century, 1996)

Sheehan, William, *British Voices from the Irish War of Independence 1916-1922* (Collins Press, 2005)

Smith, Steve, *3-2-1 Bomb Gone: Fighting Terrorist Bombers in Northern Ireland* (Sutton, 2005)

Spencer, William, *Air Force Records: A Guide for Family Historians* (Bloomsbury Academic, 2008)

Stone, David, *Cold War Warriors: The Story of the Duke of Edinburgh's Royal Regiment 1959-1994* (Pen & Sword, 1998)

Taylor, Peter, *Provos: The IRA and Sinn Fein* (Bloomsbury, 1997)

Urban, Mark, *Big Boys Rules* (Faber & Faber, 1992)

Warner, Guy, *Army Aviation in Ulster* (Colourpoint, 2004)

Warner, Guy, *First in the Field: 651 Squadron Army Air Corps* (Pen & Sword, 2011)

Warner, Guy, *Sycamores Over Ulster* (Ulster Aviation Society, 2013)

Wharton, Ken, *A Long Long War* (Helion & Company, 2008)

Wharton, Ken, *Wasted Years Wasted Lives: The British Army in Northern Ireland Volume 2 1978-1979* (Helion & Company, 2014)

Wragg, David, *Helicopters at War* (Robert Hale Ltd, 1983)

Newspapers, Magazines and Journals

Army Air Corps Journal
Belfast Telegraph
Daily Express
Daily Telegraph
DERR Journal
Fermanagh Herald
Flight International
Glasgow Herald
The Guardian
The Independent

Irish Echo
Irish Independent
Irish Press
Irish Times
The Morning Call
New York Times
RAF Historical Society Journal
Republican News/An Phoblacht
The Scotsman
Sun Sentinel
Sunday Times
The Times
Tulsa World
Ulster Herald

Archives and Official Documents

Army Incident Reports (dated: 15 December 1972, 11 September 1979, 8 May 1981, 21 July 1982, 25 May 1985, 9 January 1993)

Board of Inquiry Report into crash of Gazelle XX404

Board of Inquiry Report into shooting down of Lynx ZE380

Future Terrorist Trends (MoD, 1979)

Operation Banner: An Analysis of British Military Operations in Northern Ireland (MoD, 2006)

Extracts of RAF No.230 Squadron Operations Record Book; June 1993 and July 1994 (RAF Air Historical Branch)

Extracts of RAF No.72 Squadron Operations Record Book; December 1989, February 1990, January 1991 and May 1992 (RAF Air Historical Branch)

National Archives (UK):

CAB 129/144/7 (Memorandum by the Minister of Defence for Administration, 28 July 1969)

CAB 129/181 (Defence Estimates statement, 25 February 1975)

DEFE 24/1945 ('Armed Helicopters in Northern Ireland', 20 March-29 May 1973)

WO 141/44 (Memorandum from Air Chief Marshal Sir Hugh Trenchard, 9 October 1920)

WO/373/183 (Recommendation for Award of Air Force Cross to Major Samuel Drennan, March 1990)

AIR 27/2705 (RAF No.118 Squadron Operations Record Book, February 1960)

AIR 27/3454 (RAF No.72 Squadron Operations Record Book, August 1979)
AIR 27/3588 (RAF No.72 Squadron Operations Record Book, July/August 1982)
AIR 27/3685 (RAF No.72 Squadron Operations Record Book and Hostile Action Report, May/June 1983)
PREM 19/82 ('Appointment of Northern Ireland Security Co-ordinator')
PREM 19/279 ('South Armagh Security Review 1980')
National Archives Ireland:
Reference: 2004/7/2686 ('British Request for Permission to Overfly Border', 6 May 1973)
Reference: 2005/7/664 (Memo from Merlyn Rees to Garret FitzGerald, 13 February 1976)
Public Record Office Northern Ireland:
CENT /1/5/5 (Northern Ireland Office memo 'Paramilitary organisation in Northern Ireland', 13 February 1976)

Audio Interviews

Johnston, Mike (BBC Radio Ulster, January 2016)
Booth, Michael (IWM tape 33200)
Forde, Martin (IWM tape 33894)
Glaze, John (IWM tape 30108)
Lawton, Christopher (IWM tape 28698)
Thompson, Julian (IWM tape 28361)
Turner, Ray (IWM tape 30025)

Websites

www.airdisplaymuseum.co.uk
www.thebrokenelbow.com
www.bureauofmilitaryhistory.ie
www.cain.ulst.ac.uk: Conflict and Politics in Northern Ireland
www.fleetairarmoa.org: Fleet Air Arm Officers Association
www.flyingmarines.com
www.hansard.parliament.uk
www.instre.org: Institute of the Royal Engineers
www.jsbni.com: Judicial Studies Board for Northern Ireland
www.margaretthatcherfoundation.org
www.oireachtas.ie: National Parliament of Ireland

Index